About the Author

Phil Merrick is the founder of Peoplemad Ltd, a Fellow of the Institute of Leadership Management, an Advisory Board Member of the Youth Charter, a Business Mentor for Business Wales and a former senior executive with one of the biggest banks in Europe.

He has a track record of building high performing teams and has spent a great deal of his career in trouble shooting roles helping businesses improve performance, particularly through the organisation and management of people. Phil is now focused on helping people improve performance using the Peoplemad Success Model © which he has developed to make the process easier for people.

Phil loves all sports, especially football, is a passionate Leeds United supporter and lives in North Wales with his wife Sian and has three daughters Gemma, Hannah and Kate.

Dedication

This book will challenge the way you think about yourself.... and other people.

For my dear mum Betty who taught me
to respect other people.
At least those who deserve it.

Phil Merrick

The •peoplemad success model

Be the best: you, your team, your business
The essential handbook for improving performance

Copyright © Phil Merrick (2016)

The right of Phil Merrick to be identified as author of this work has been asserted by his in accordance with section 77 and 78 of the Copyright, Designs and Patents Act 1988.

All rights reserved. No part of this publication may be reproduced, stored in a retrieval system, or transmitted in any form or by any means, electronic, mechanical, photocopying, recording, or otherwise, without the prior permission of the publishers.

Any person who commits any unauthorized act in relation to this publication may be liable to criminal prosecution and civil claims for damages.

A CIP catalogue record for this title is available from the British Library.

ISBN 9781786128881 (Paperback)
ISBN 9781786128898 (Hardback)
ISBN 9781786128904 (E-Book)

www.austinmacauley.com

First Published (2016)
Austin Macauley Publishers Ltd.
25 Canada Square
Canary Wharf
London
E14 5LQ

Is a registered trademark.

Acknowledgments

My thanks go to:

- The many managers that I've had the pleasure of working for - you can learn as much from the bad ones as you can the good ones.
- My colleagues and friends in the many teams I've been involved in – so much skill, knowledge and experience and importantly camaraderie.
- Tony Buzan. I first came across his book 'Make the Most of Your Mind' in 1981 and it inspired me to find out more about how to improve performance through reading more effectively, improving memory, solving problems more easily and thinking creatively. All this was a relatively new concept at the time and he went on to write many more books, including 'Mind Maps'. I had the pleasure of meeting him for lunch twenty years later and asked him to sign my very first Buzan book. Ironically he wrote his message and signature in four different colours, one of his many tips on how to remember things – we think in pictures so use lots of colour in your notes. You'll notice from this handbook that I still value his advice.
- My wife Sian and three lovely daughters Gemma, Hannah and Kate who have all helped shape the model with their personal experiences and invaluable feedback.
- Finally, to Vinh Tran and his design team at Austin Macauley for all their hard work in formatting and editing the manuscript.

The •peoplemad success model

Believe in yourself
Surround yourself with the right people
Keep things simple

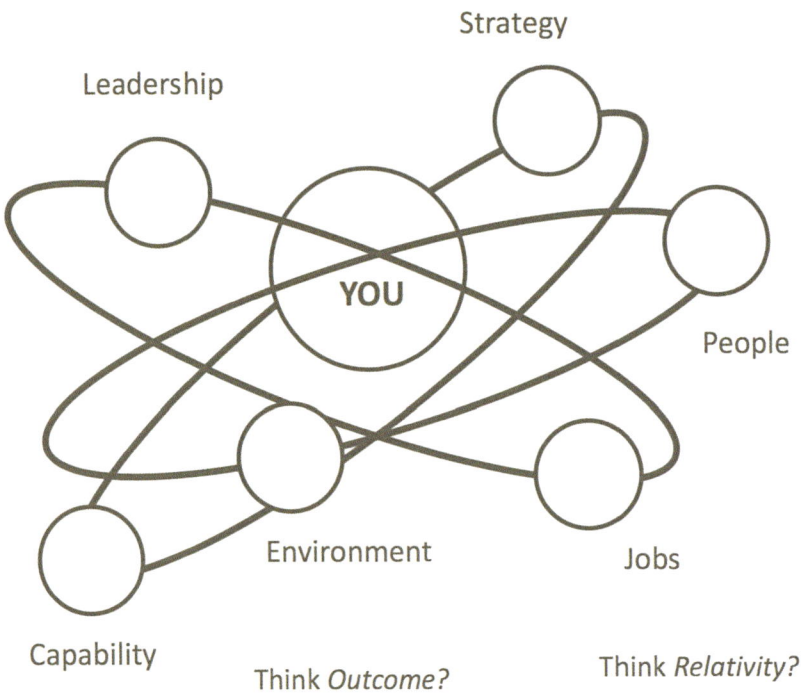

•peoplemad © Phil Merrick

Contents

1. Introduction
2. You are the centre of your universe
3. Develop your strategy
4. Surround yourself with the right people
5. Get the right people doing the right things
6. Create the right environment
7. Build your own capability
8. Display Leadership
9. The •**peoplemad** tool kit
10. How you can use •**peoplemad**
11. A quick summary

'Believe in the best, think your best, study your best, have a goal for your best, never be satisfied with less than your best, try your best, and in the long run things will turn out for the best.'
Henry Ford, American motor manufacturer.

1. Introduction

- **•peoplemad** is about creating capability, getting things done and improving performance - being the best at what you do.

- It is entirely about people – how good we are and how good we could be if we deployed ourselves and the people we work with properly.

- It will help to improve your own performance as well as that of your team – whether it's in sport, business or life in general.

- It starts with you – lead by example and get skilled at dealing with people.

- This is a concept based on over 30 years experience reviewing business practice and building high performing teams.

- **•peoplemad** is easy to understand, easy to remember and easy to implement.

- Some people will do parts of it already and do it well.

- The trick is to do all of it and do it really well.

A personal note from the author:

This model is based very much on personal experience so I'm going to tell you a little about my background.

I've had a very successful career which has allowed me to do lots of interesting things – but I'll state up front that it hasn't been easy and I've had to make some very difficult decisions along the way.

Importantly I've worked with some great people who have all contributed towards my career.

My first job was with the First National City Bank of New York, which lasted 2 days – because I hadn't told my mum or my University that I was fed up of being a student. I then joined the Nat West in Rhyl, which lasted 18 months because they wanted to move me to London. In those days that was the deal, it felt very much like the bank owned your career and to get on you had to move around the country. So I left… thinking that me and the banking world were just not suited for each other. It's ironic that thirty odd years later I was on the Executive Committee of Bank of Scotland Corporate Asset Finance responsible for over 8 billion pounds worth of assets.

So going back to 1974….completely disenchanted with banking I joined Clwyd Health Authority. I liked it and it suited my lifestyle at the time and whilst there were a few promotions, the issue for me was that it didn't matter how hard I worked or how dedicated I was, I never felt that I was being fairly rewarded.

So with a small family and a large mortgage I had to find other ways of supplementing my income. Some money came from playing football and we started a milk round business. Every morning I'd get up at 5am and deliver milk before going off to work – 7 days a week. At weekends I'd collect the money before going off to play football.

I tried everything. I wrote my first book A Game of Two Halves and I invented a board game. I took the prototype down to Canary

Wharf in London and managed to persuade a buyer at WH Smiths to order 150 games for their Oxford Street store to see if it would sell. At that time my business knowledge was very limited. I was learning as much as I could from books and I just felt that it was too much of a risk to try and raise the huge amount of capital that was needed to put the game into production. So I didn't do it.

Then came one of those pivotal moments that happens in your career; sometimes decisions get forced upon you… I was badly injured playing football. This meant I didn't get my football money and my wife Sian had to do the milk round. She was 8 months pregnant with Kate, we already had Gemma and Hannah who were still very young …and of course a mortgage to pay.

I referred earlier to having to make some big decisions, well it was now time to make one. I gave up football, which really hurt, stopped the milk business and tried to find a career that paid me what I was worth.

At that time Computer Auditing was just becoming fashionable, if that's the right word, so I took a computer audit exam with the Institute of Internal Auditors and applied for 9 different jobs all over the country. I had interviews with the Stock Exchange, British Rail and NWS Bank who were the first to offer me a job.

At that time NWS had a bad reputation for getting rid of people when they didn't perform, so it was a huge risk. But I decided to go for it and the move to the corporate world was just what I needed. In fact I thrived on it. I was 35 when I joined, after 4 years I was Assistant General Manager with NWS Bank, 6 years after that I became a General Manager with the Bank of Scotland and 5 years after that I was a Senior Executive with HBOS. At that time there were 74,000 people in the HBOS Group and just 27 executives who were on a higher grade than me.

I'd never considered myself to be a 'Banker'. I was in the industry but my roles were all about setting things up, checking that things worked properly and changing things for the better.

My senior positions included Head of Group Audit and Consultancy for Capital Bank, Head of Business Banking Strategy for the Bank of Scotland and Head of Corporate Programme management for HBOS managing portfolios worth 100's of millions of pounds.

Operationally I've set up and managed successful businesses as well as running a large scale operations unit of over 1500 staff. Everything from front end sales through to back office collections.

A great deal of the knowledge and experience used in **•peoplemad** however has come from trouble shooting roles running small high performing teams.
These teams have been involved in numerous business reviews, acquisitions, disposals, restructures and mergers mainly in the UK but also in Ireland, France, Austria, Australia and New Zealand. Managing change across different countries and different cultures. The common denominator throughout has been the quest to change things for the better. I've seen it done well, by my teams and I've seen it done badly. Not by my teams of course.

On the non business side of things I've always loved sport. As mentioned I've played and managed in semi professional football and at junior level I played basketball for Wales and represented my county at cricket and athletics. So I needed to get back into it. I wrote books about football and I managed a golfer, who is now an Assistant PGA professional and also a motor racing driver, the 2013 British Formula Ford Motor Racing Champion and 2015 & 16 Porsche Carrera Cup Champion.
I spent 2 years as Chairman of Prestatyn Town FC. We won the Welsh Cup and got into Europe and we made football history by being the first Welsh club to get into the next round of the Europa League at the first attempt. But it was voluntary and it was starting to take over my life. If I do something I want to do it properly so this is where I needed to make another one of those big decisions: **•peoplemad** or Prestatyn Town FC?... unfortunately there wasn't room for both.
So I handed in my notice at the club to focus my efforts entirely on **•peoplemad**. I've been writing this book and developing the model on and off for 5 years now so it's about time I did something with it. Here it is at last… and I hope you like it.

•peoplemad is designed to…

- Improve performance from day one.

- Be used by everyone, everywhere, whatever you do.

- Simplify extensive and sometimes complex subject matter.

- Unite your team in the pursuit of strategy/common goals.

- Get everyone to the same level of understanding of key business knowledge.

- Be a 'must have' tool for managers and staff.

- Re-energise and give everyone a boost to get on and achieve things.

- Give everyone a sense of ownership of their lives and career.

- Provide a foundation for the future.

There is one key learning point that underpins everything else in this book: **Surround yourself with the right people.**

This is critical in life as much as it is in business.

•peoplemad can be used for just about anything

- Develop individuals in their quest for improved performance.
- Continually enhance your own performance and leadership skills.
- Set things up from scratch starting with the need for a vision through to creating the right environment and the development of your people.
- Review existing operations to identify weaknesses and improve performance.

>   Business planning
>   Reviewing and improving performance
>   Current state assessments
>   Setting up a new business venture
>   Troubleshooting
>   Project and change management
>   Managing teams
>   Management audits
>   Recruitment
>   Career management
>   Personal life management

This is covered in more detail in Section 10

How to use this book

- This handbook is a source of reference that you can carry around with you at all times.

- Refer to the quick summary in Section 11 as a reminder on the model, the rules and the thinking tools.

- Use it as a work book – add your own notes, record your own experiences.

- You can read it from cover to cover in page number order or jump freely from one section to another.

- It is colour coded for easy reference.

- One of the benefits of the model is that all the points are linked and cross referenced using the coloured planet icons. Some subjects e.g. planning are covered in more than one section to help with continuity.

- The points in this book have been stripped down to their basic elements; the logic has purposely been over simplified and explained as key messages in bullet point format.

- The format follows one of the important •**peoplemad** rules – keep things simple.

The key sections are colour coded

- You are the centre of your universe
- Develop your strategy
- Get the right people
- Do the right things
- Create the right environment
- Build your own capability
- Display leadership

Some points about the methodology…

- **It is designed for you to use both personally and professionally.**
- It makes you think about things differently.
- It provides a methodology.
- It gives you some tools. Learn to:
    Determine the outcomes you want
    Look at everything relative to everything else
    Focus on the future and how you get there
    Prioritise tasks effectively
- It packages together lots of knowledge and experience.
- It uses opinion on best practice.
- It challenges you to think about yourself and your relationships with other people.
- **It puts you at the very heart of the model.**
- Note: The methodology supports the technical knowledge that is required for professional practitioners and does not attempt to replace it – e.g. Project Management.

To improve performance you have to be prepared to change. Change requires a move from one state to another – this particularly applies to your state of mind..

●peoplemad is very much about you managing your state of mind.

Life and •peoplemad

- **You**
- **People**
- **Outcome**

In it's simplest form, life is about you, your relationships with other people and the various outcomes that happen as a result. That's all there is.

•peoplemad is about you taking control and improving those outcomes.

Decide the outcome you want.

Improve your capability and learn how to work with and get the best out of other people in order to achieve it.

Get into the habit of thinking 'What OUTCOME do I want?' You can then work backwards to see how you are going to achieve it. This way of thinking is very powerful, you can apply it to anything and is included in the tool kit in Section 9.

This stamp is used throughout the handbook as a reminder – make sure your actions deliver the right outcomes.

The power of people

- Man has achieved a great deal in his short time on this planet with seemingly limited resources – he has created wondrous things from what started as an endless expanse of water, rock and vegetation.

- Today we put people into space (and bring them back again), we communicate with people on the other side of our planet in a matter of seconds and we transplant human organs with an amazing rate of success.

- We make the world go round, we are powerful creatures and when we put our mind to it we can do amazing things.

- Harness this power – get the right people doing the right things performing at their peak and you, your team and your business can achieve great success.

'The people with whom you share your life affect your happiness and your success – choose them wisely.' **Phil Merrick.**

The •peoplemad success model

Albert Einstein's picture is here for two good reasons.

You will see on the next few pages that the •**peoplemad** model uses the analogy of our solar system to explain the methodology and importantly your role in it.

Naturally Einstein creates the link and will help you remember the following points:

1. Einstein said that doing the same thing over and over again and expecting different results is a sign of madness. It follows then that to improve performance (moving from where you are today to where you want to be tomorrow) you need to do something differently. This particularly applies to the way you think – improving performance and being successful is very much about the application of thought. How you think is critical in helping you achieve your goals.

2. One way of thinking that will help improve performance is Relativity Thinking. Everything is relative to everything else. 'Being the best' is a relative statement and you will only be the best if you are better than everyone else. It's an obvious statement but this thinking is important whenever you are looking at the different elements of your performance or those of your team. Also, no matter how well you perform you will always need to consider the competition, both internally within your team and externally from the opposition. This is covered in more detail in the •**peoplemad** tool kit in Section 9.

The •peoplemad success model

So let's move on to the model... and it's about you.
You are at the heart of it – you control everything. Think of yourself as the ring master. In charge and in control.

I wanted to create something that makes life easier for people so the model has been designed in this format so that it's easy to understand, easy to remember and importantly easy to implement.

The model is drawn as a solar system. The key elements are represented by the sun and 6 planets each with 5 moons. The details of each planet and their moons are explained in separate sections. It's designed this way so it works well pictorially which helps when you're trying to remember the model. We think in pictures and when things are colourful it helps. A model gives structure and order on which to build knowledge so the solar system is a very powerful analogy representing science, space and life itself.

In our solar system everything revolves around the sun. In •peoplemad everything revolves around you. This is your universe – you are in control.

An important point is that it works well as a model – using all the components to improve whatever it is you are using it for. It's also a mind set and as you start using it you will realise that you can apply it to anything.

The •peoplemad success model

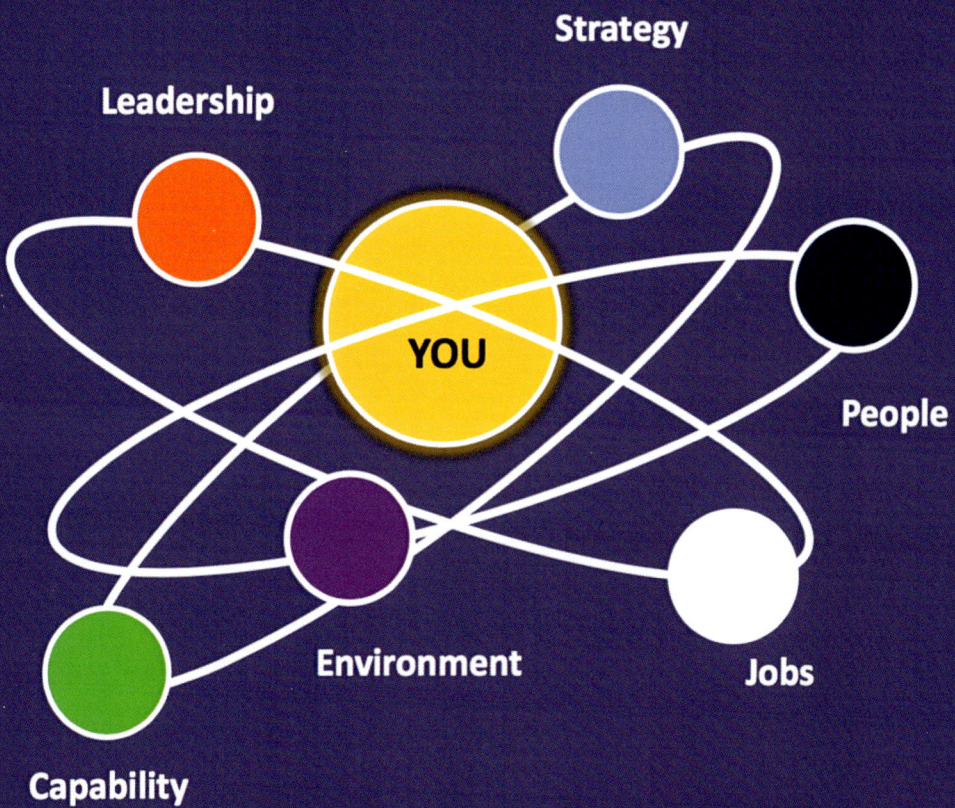

•peoplemad © Phil Merrick

Each planet has 5 moons

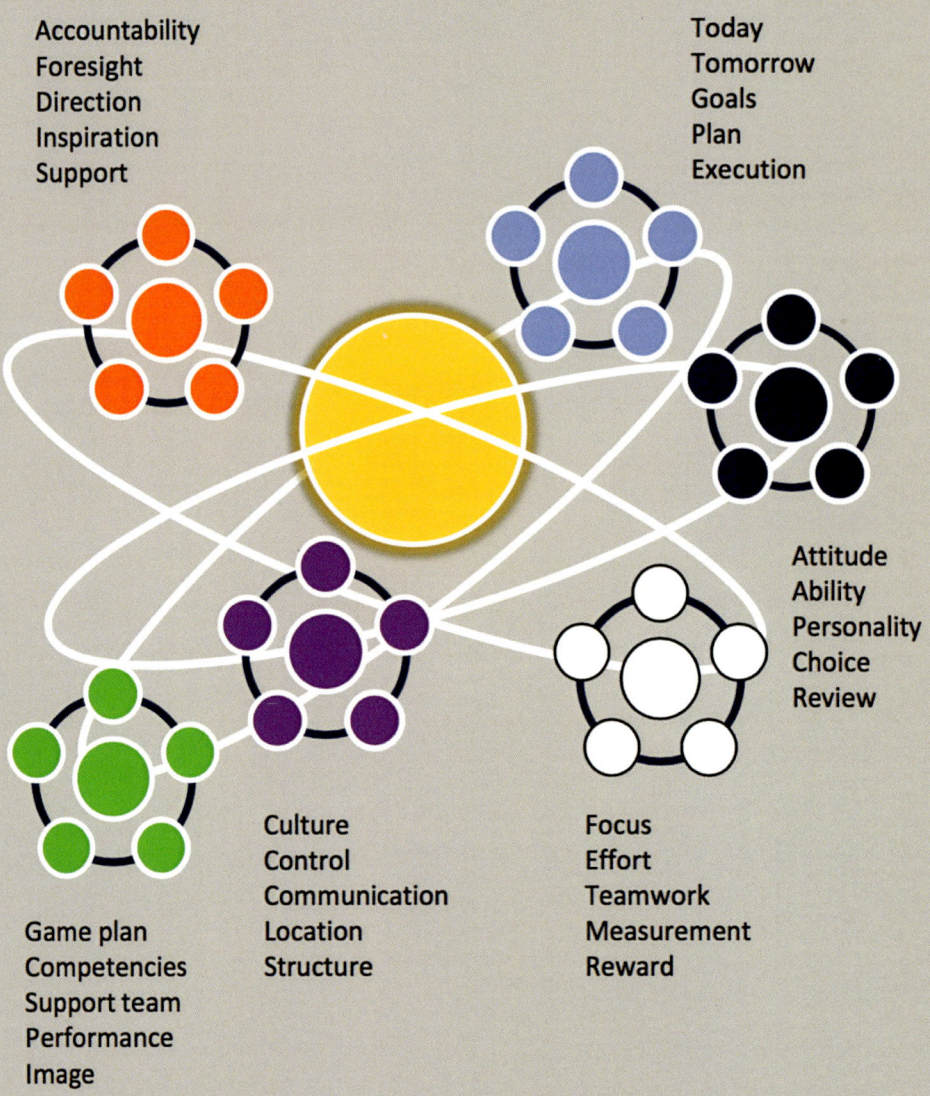

Overview of the •peoplemad success model

Use the 6 planets as the key components:
- Develop your strategy.
- Surround yourself with the right people.
- Get the right people doing the right things.
- Create the right environment.
- Build your own capability.
- Display leadership.

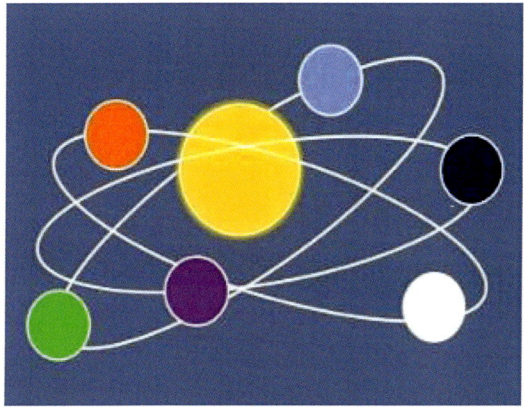

In very simple terms:
- Know what you're aiming to achieve and get the right people on board.
- Get them doing the right things in an environment that will allow them to flourish and perform at their very best.
- Build your own capability and display strong leadership at all times.

A formula to become the best...

	You need	Your team needs	Your business needs
A strategy - a vision and a plan	✓	✓	✓
The right people to help you	✓	✓	✓
Everyone doing the right things focused on your vision	✓	✓	✓
The right environment to enable everyone to perform at their best	✓	✓	✓
You trying to be the best you can be	✓	✓	✓
You and your colleagues leading the challenge to be the best	✓	✓	✓

•peoplemad © Phil Merrick

The •peoplemad success model

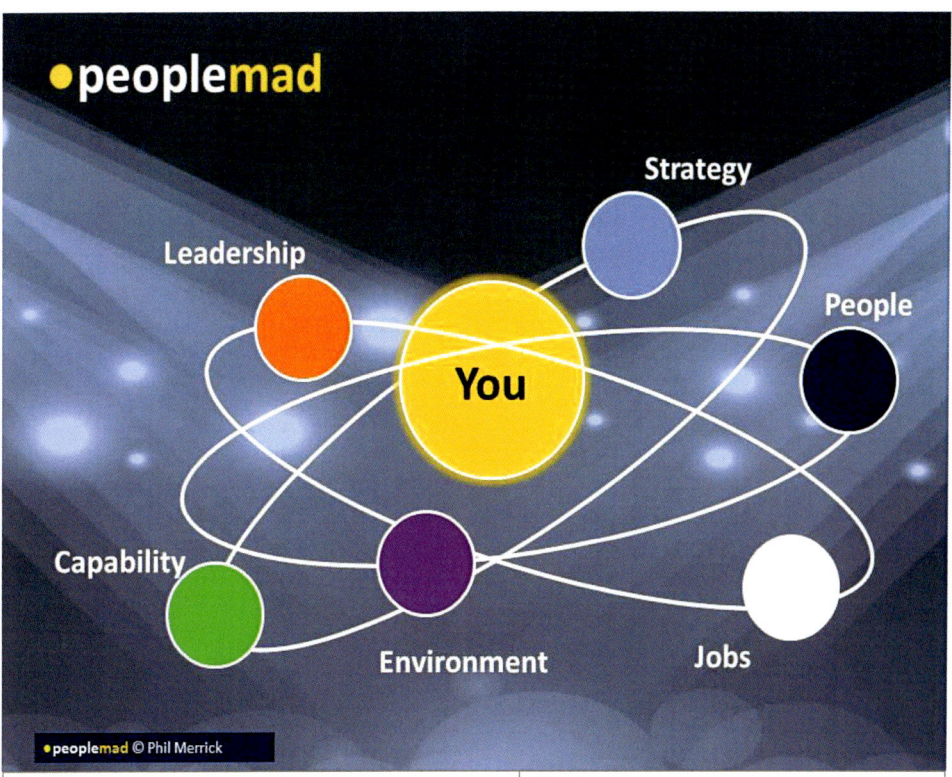

Notes	Action

Your own •**peoplemad** notes

The •peoplemad success model

2. You are the centre of your universe

In this section:
- The •**peoplemad** success model
- Believe in yourself
- Surround yourself with the right people
- Keep things simple
- Your own •**peoplemad** notes
- You are at the centre of everything
- A philosophical view
- You are in control
- Your own •**peoplemad** notes

'Life is about choices. Everyday you make choices that affect your livelihood. You can choose to stay in bed in the morning or get up and take on the World.'
Phil Merrick.

How to build your capability and develop your leadership skills are covered in Sections 7 & 8.

The •peoplemad success model

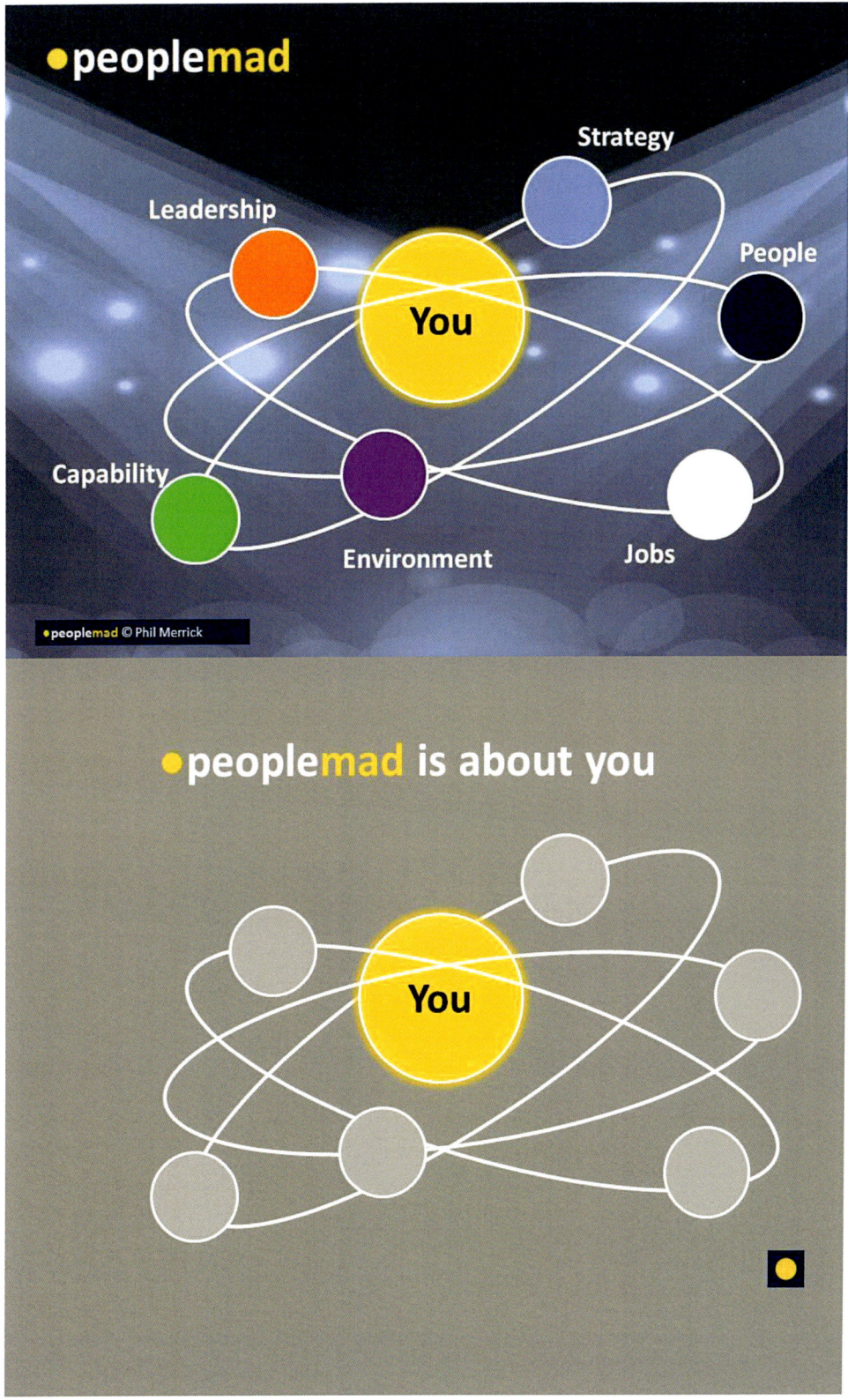

The •peoplemad success model

The 3 rules of •peoplemad
1. Believe in yourself

- I'm a big believer in having a positive attitude. Not to the detriment of reality – I don't believe for a second that everything is pink and fluffy.
- I'm positive because I believe you can make things happen.
- Most of what happens in life is of your own making.
- Don't make excuses, don't blame your circumstances and certainly don't blame other people. (You'll read this a lot in this handbook).
- How can you expect other people to believe in you if you don't believe in yourself?

- Attitude is everything.
- You can achieve what you believe.

- What would you do if you knew you couldn't fail?
- What would you do if you didn't care what people think? Would you do things differently. What's stopping you?

'One of the greatest principles is that men can do what they think they can do.'
Norman Vincent Peale, American writer and minister.

 2. Surround yourself with the right people

- No matter how self motivated or independent you are you need other people.
- You rely on other people every day of your life. Thousands of actions taken by friends, relatives, customers, politicians, employers, colleagues, suppliers, coaches, teachers etc impact your life and how you feel.
- How many bad days have you had because the bus was late, a delivery didn't arrive, the builder didn't turn up on time or you were late for work because of those infernal road works?
- The better other people are at doing their jobs the better your life will be.
- This is particularly evident in a team situation where you are dependant on your colleagues.
- If you are in a management position your performance will be determined by how well other people do their jobs.
- People are powerful creatures, we communicate, we create things, have ideas, make decisions, we make things happen. We influence other people.
- Other people have attributes that you don't have – why not use their skills to complement yours.
- The power of many is a lot more than the power of one.

3. Keep things simple

- Things that are overcomplicated can be difficult to understand and even more difficult to explain to someone else.
- The more complex something is then the more chance there is of it going wrong and the more difficult and costly it will be to put right.
- Things do not have to be complicated to be effective – very often it's the opposite.
- If you've read any of Tom Peters' books you will know that he's very much about quality and he believes that almost all quality improvement comes from simplification of design, manufacturing, layout, processes and procedures.
- Keeping things simple especially needs to be applied to communication which needs clarity and understanding for it to be effective.
- De-clutter your life. Get rid of things that are not important or get in the way.

'Never invest in any idea you can't illustrate with a crayon.' **Peter Lynch, Wall Street Investor.**

The •peoplemad success model

- **Believe in yourself**

- **Surround yourself with the right people**

- **Keep things simple** Make life easier

•peoplemad © Phil Merrick

Notes	Action

Your own •peoplemad notes

The •peoplemad success model

 ## You are at the centre of everything

- Everything revolves around you.
- You are in control of your thoughts and actions.
- You decide what you do, no-one else.
- Other people affect your happiness and success – learn how to choose them, learn how to deal with them.
- You decide what you do with your life and your career, don't rely on other people to do it for you - other people have their own lives and careers to worry about.
- How you deal with other people will determine how other people deal with you.
- Take ownership
    - Don't make excuses
    - Don't blame other people
    - Don't put up barriers
- Be self aware
    - Think about what you do
    - Assess how well you do it
- If things aren't working out do something about it.
- Get the best people on your side.
- Get on with it and make things happen.

Whoopi Goldberg, American actress said: *'I am where I am because I believe in all possibilities.'*

A philosophical view ...

- You are the centre of your own universe.
- You control your own thoughts and your own actions.
- You have your own beliefs, objectives and ways of doing things.
- There are 7 billion other people doing exactly the same.
- There will be 10 billion long before the end of this century.
- Lives are bound to clash.
- There will be conflict.
- There will be accidents.
- There will be competition for what you are trying to do.

Accept this is how it works, that's life. Your success will come from how you deal with it.

- **Learn to understand:**

    –how other people think
    –how other people behave
    –the impact you have on other people

- It makes sense to be really good at dealing with people.

You are in control

You control how you think

Everything is in your head. Everything. Your ideas, your emotions, your beliefs, your worries, your memories. Your whole life is played out inside your head and you have the power to determine how you live it. You decide who you listen to, what you read and what you believe. You have complete freedom over what you think.

Your whole life is played out inside your head.

You control how you behave

You control your behaviour. No-one else. The actions that you take and the things that you say are entirely within your control. How you react to different situations and how you treat other people is entirely down to you. Life is about making choices, success is about making the right choices. You decide whether you get up in the morning and take on the World or stay in bed. It's your life, it's your choice.

The •peoplemad success model

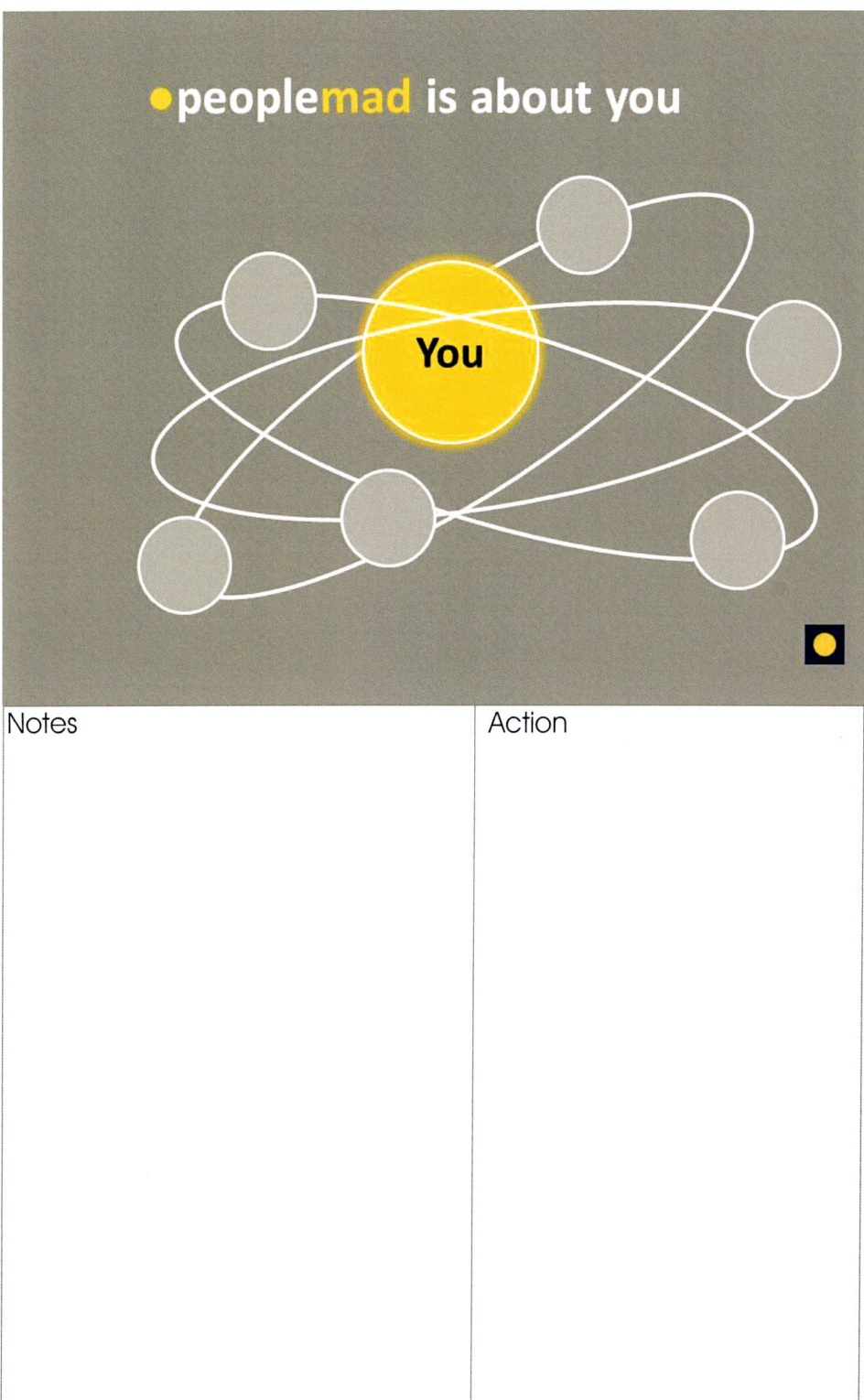

Notes

Action

Your own •peoplemad notes

The •peoplemad success model

3. Develop your strategy

In this section:

- The •**peoplemad** success model
- Develop your strategy
- Strategy in simple terms…
- Be clear what you want…
- Know where you are today
- Current State Assessment
- Know where you want to be tomorrow
- Vision
- Involve other people…
- Set your goals
- Goals
- Develop your plan
- Plan
- Planning is easy
- Pause and reflect
- Brown paper planning
- Measure progress
- Execution is critical
- Execution
- Impact on other people
- Your own •**peoplemad** notes

The •peoplemad success model

•peoplemad

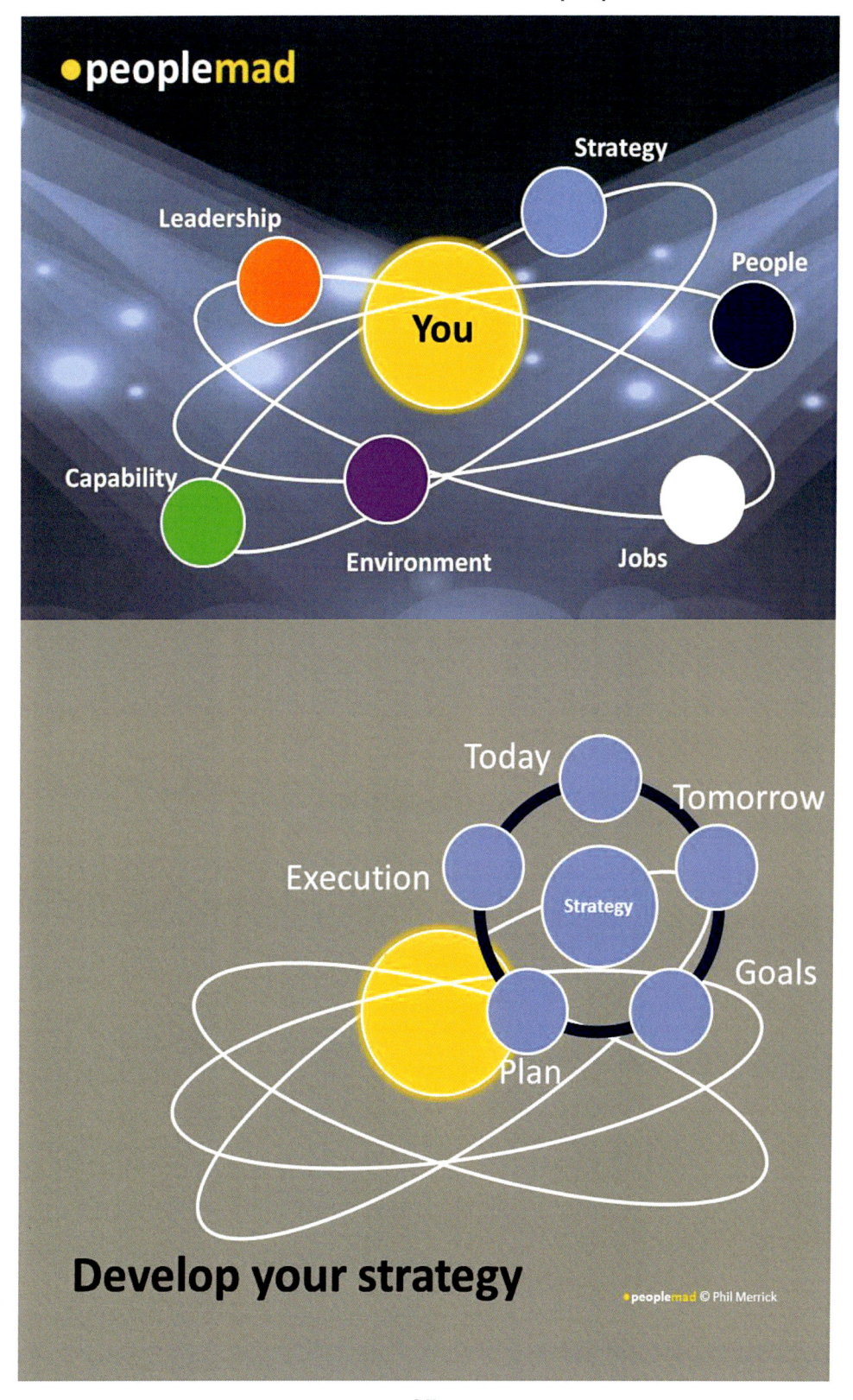

Strategy
Leadership
People
You
Capability
Environment
Jobs

Today
Tomorrow
Execution
Strategy
Goals
Plan

Develop your strategy

•peoplemad © Phil Merrick

Develop your strategy

You don't jump on a bus without knowing where you're going and what time you're likely to arrive so that should be the same with your business… or sports team… or your career.

Do you have a vision? Are you excited by it? Are you passionate about it? Importantly are your team excited by It? If they are and they believe in what you're doing as an organisation then you're a long way towards having a happy workforce. People perform better when they feel good about themselves and feeling part of what is going on and contributing is very motivational.

Of course you need a plan.

A vision without a plan is nothing but a dream.

You will be able to get your plan from a gap analysis between the picture you draw about today, known as current state and the one you draw about tomorrow – your vision. List the things you need to change put them in some sort of order and this will be your plan of action.
Importantly be honest with yourself about what life looks like today. If you pretend things are better or worse than they really are then you will not come up with the right list of things that need attention or be able to accurately prioritise the things to tackle first.

Strategy in simple terms…

Knowing where you are today, knowing where you want to be tomorrow and having a plan to get there.

- Picture the future – your vision.

- What will success look like? Define what the future will look like in figures and pictures. Show what you will achieve with your strategy.

- Check today's position – your current state assessment.

- Devise how you can move from today's position to achieve your future vision – your strategy.

- Set yourself some targets and objectives.

- Work out what you are going to do and when – your plan.

- Put your plan into action – the execution.

Note: Execution. You can have the best strategy in the World but it is a complete waste of time if it's not carried out properly. Make sure you get the right people, doing the right things, in the right environment; which of course is a fundamental part of the ●**peoplemad** model.

The •peoplemad success model

Be clear what you want and how you are going to get it

- If you want to achieve anything in life then you need to have a pretty good idea about what it is you want.

- Every business should have a vision of where it wants to be in the future and a strategy showing how it's going to get there.

- It is the same for individuals. You won't be able to plan where you want to be in a few years time if you don't have a vision of where that place is and what it looks like.

- Think of it like a journey. You know where you're starting from and you know where you want to get to. Plan how you are going to get there and how long it should take you.

- The better you can picture it, articulate it and describe it in writing then the easier it will be to achieve.

- The trick is to do the right amount of research and soul searching to be absolutely certain that your vision is what you really want.

- Decide what you want, work out how you are going to achieve it and make it happen.

- **Don't give up until you've done it.**

The •peoplemad success model

Today ✓ Tomorrow
Execution
Strategy
Goals
Plan

•peoplemad © Phil Merrick

Know where you are today

Vision

Where you want to be tomorrow

Where you are today

**Current state assessment
Accurate facts and figures
Assess everything**

Current State Assessment

Knowing where you are today:

- See Section 7 for ideas on personal strategy.
- Carry out a review – a current state assessment.
- Understand today's position in as much detail as possible. For businesses this might include strengths, weaknesses, markets, products, customers, staff, systems, costs, income streams etc.
- Assess everything including people and their feelings.
- Get accurate facts and figures.
- Be truthful as to the realistic position.
- The more accurate and detailed the information the easier it will be to make decisions on what needs to change.
- This is about today – forget any current plans to change things, don't cloud the issue with what might happen in the next few days, weeks, months.
- Think of it as a snapshot in time.

'If you don't know where you are, your true situation, then you are lost from the outset. You cannot plot a course forward if you don't know where you are starting from.' **Sir Terry Leahy, Tesco.**

The •peoplemad success model

Today
Tomorrow
Execution
Strategy
Goals
Plan

•peoplemad © Phil Merrick

Know where you want to be tomorrow

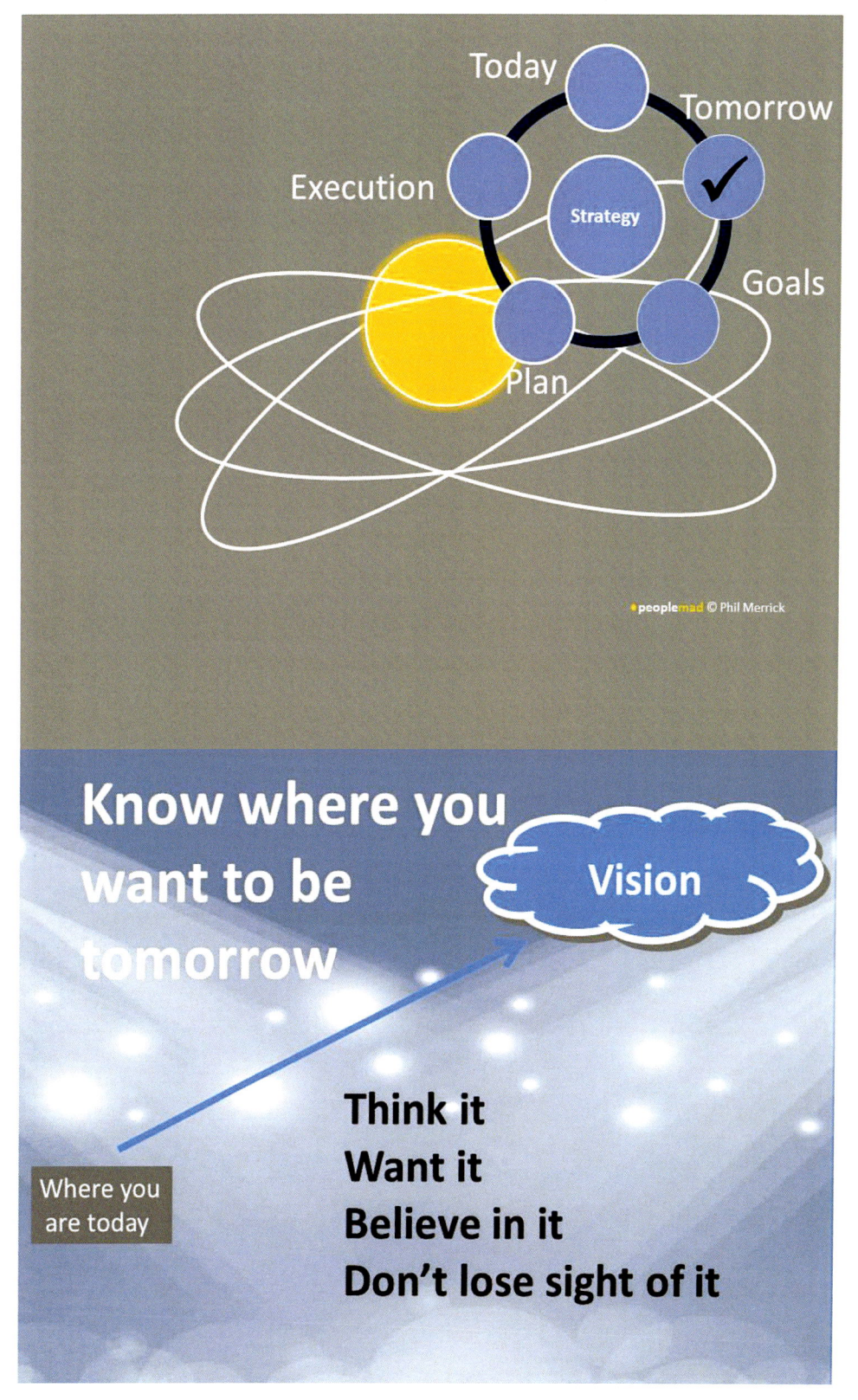

Vision

Where you are today

**Think it
Want it
Believe in it
Don't lose sight of it**

The •peoplemad success model

Vision

Think OUTCOME

- Aspire, desire, dream.
- Open your mind.
- Don't put restrictions on your thoughts.
- Believe you can do anything that you believe you can do.
- Research it.
- Draw it, paint it, write it down.
- Give it as much detail as possible.
- Sleep on it.
- Close your eyes and paint it in your mind.

Check and rationalise –
- Are you passionate about it?
- Can you get excited by it?
- Why are you doing it?
- Is it within reach? It doesn't have to be easy but it needs to feel achievable to keep you motivated.

'The indispensable first step to getting the things you want out of life is this: decide what you want.'
Ben Stein, American lawyer, actor and comedian.

The •peoplemad success model

Think it
See it
Draw it
Write it
Want it

Vision

Believe it

Don't lose sight of it

Involve other people…

- Start with your vision.

- Think of the people who will help you realise your vision.

- Do you need to involve people who will be impacted by your strategy? This will depend on how they are impacted.

- Brainstorm ideas.

- Take your thoughts and drawings and turn them into detailed descriptions of what the future looks like.

- Remember to consider all the areas reviewed in the current state assessment.

- Plot how to move from today's position to the vision.

- Get commitment and support as early as possible.

- Assess the risks and put mitigation plans in place.

'Imagination is more important than knowledge.'

'If at first the idea is not absurd. Then there is no hope for it.'
Albert Einstein, German born American physicist.

'With our thoughts we make the World.'
Buddha, Indian religious teacher and founder of Buddhism.

'The past cannot be changed. The future is yet in your power.'
Mary Pickford, American silent screen actress.

The •peoplemad success model

Set your goals

Think OUTCOME

Objective 4
Objective 3
Objective 2
Objective 1

Where you are today

Where you want to be tomorrow

SMART
Right OUTCOME
Stepping stones

Goals

Think OUTCOME

- The Oxford English Dictionary definition is: an aim or a desired result.
- You now have a vision and a strategy – setting goals will give focus to make it happen.
- In many businesses the terms goals, objectives and targets are often used interchangeably. For simplicity in this handbook the term 'goals' is used to describe the desired outcome and is considered to be a combination of targets and objectives.
- Targets are what you are aiming for, objectives are the things you achieve along the way to help you get there.
- Keep objectives simple and attainable.
- Make sure they are the right ones and lead you down the right path.
- Describe them in such a way that there is no doubt when they are achieved.
- Set some short term objectives – they will act as stepping stones and give a sense of achievement along the way.
- Get commitment and support – think about everyone impacted by your actions.
- Communicate progress.
- Celebrate success as each objective is achieved.
- See Sections 5 & 9 for notes on measuring performance.

The •peoplemad success model

Objective 4

Objective 3

Objective 2

Objective 1

Target

Your journey

•peoplemad © Phil Merrick

The **•peoplemad** success model

Today
Tomorrow
Execution
Strategy
Goals
Plan

•peoplemad © Phil Merrick

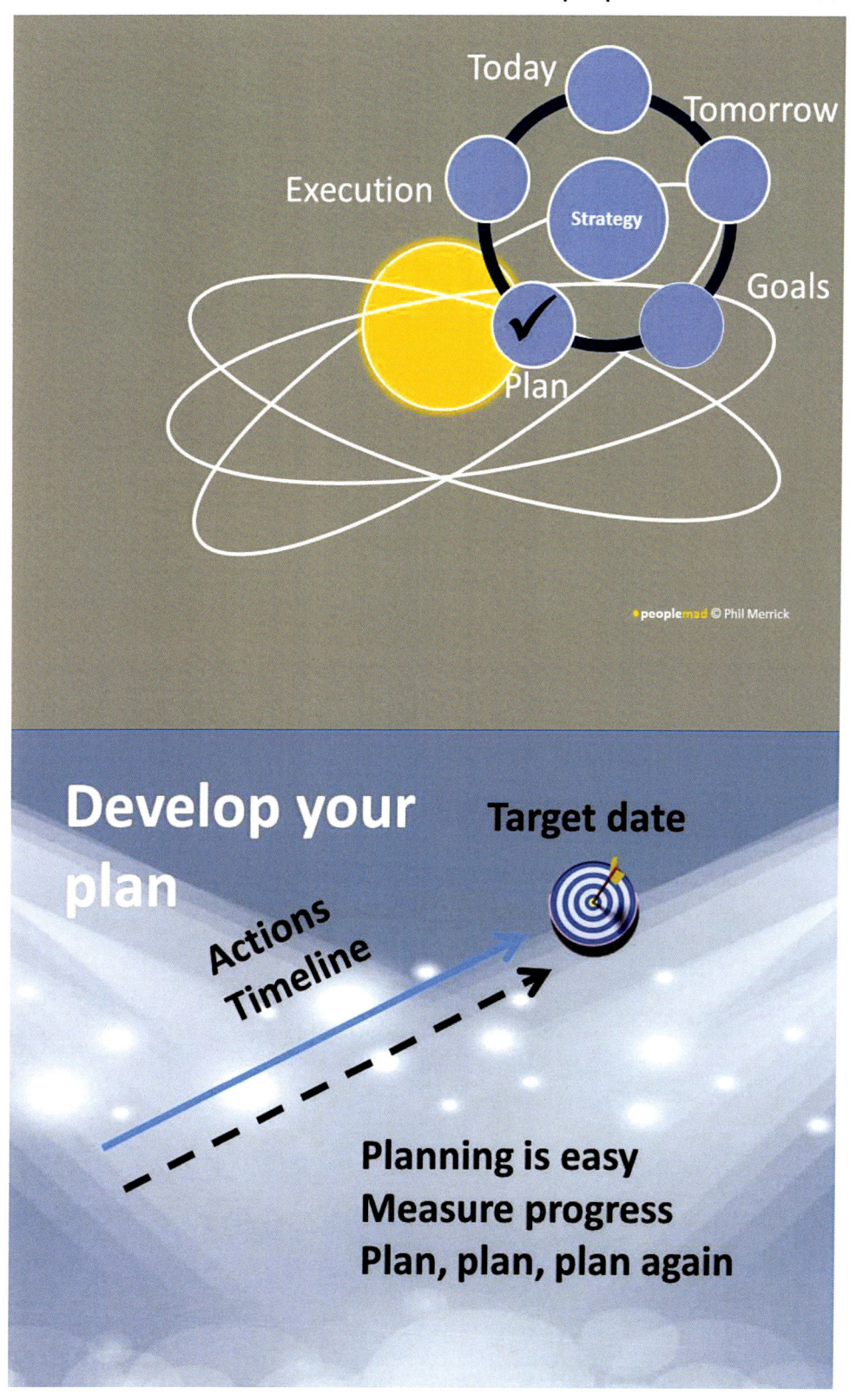

Develop your plan

Target date

Actions
Timeline

**Planning is easy
Measure progress
Plan, plan, plan again**

The •peoplemad success model

'It is a mistake to look too far ahead. Only one link of the chain of destiny can be handled at a time.'
Sir Winston Churchill, British Prime Minister.

'Focus on the future. It's no use worrying about the past. You can't change it so just learn from it. You can change the future so that's what you should focus on.' **Phil Merrick.**

Note: *strategies need to be continually reviewed in line with evolving situations.*

Plan

- Take the vision and compare with the current state to see which areas need to change.
- Make a simple plan – a list of what you are going to do and when.
- If you need the help of other people then also decide who is going to do what.
- The more people involved and the more complicated the change being undertaken then the more detailed the plan will need to be.
- Some activity will depend on other things that need to be done first – in project management these are called dependencies.
- Think of the risks involved – they will need to be managed and they take time.
- Think of the people involved – they will need to be managed and they take time ☺.
- All plans have financial implications – think costs and budgets and align financial plans to operational plans based on activity and timelines.
- Plans need to be kept up to date and communicated.
- Planning is a skill get good at it.

The •peoplemad success model

Planning is easy

Think OUTCOME

- Make a list of all the things that need to be done.
- Put them in some sort of order remembering that some things might be dependent on others (e.g. if you are building a house the walls can't be built until the foundations are in).
- Draw a timeline and put the actions that need to be taken under the appropriate dates.
- Allocate jobs to people.
- A trick is to start with the end date and work backwards. It's like planning a journey. What time do I want to get there? How long will it take? So what time do I need to leave?
- Put in some milestones – where you want to be by a certain point in time. This will help target progress and give a sense of continual achievement.
- Sit back and assess whether your plan is realistic and achievable under your timescales.
- Have I missed anything?
- What would happen if?
- Plan, plan and plan again until you are happy.

The simple trick of starting with the end date and working backwards might seem obvious but you would be surprised how many people don't do this.

Pause and reflect

- Build in some breathing space, a couple of days every month or so. It is a good discipline to sit back and check that everything is on track – there is nothing wrong with building in pauses.

- It also helps with contingency – just in case the project needs a bit more time in certain areas.

- No matter how well you plan there will be things that come out of the woodwork and affect your timelines.

- Rushing to squeeze things in might seem okay in terms of meeting your plan but it is high risk and could affect the quality of your work.

- Think about consolidation – depending on what it is you are doing there may be an occasion where you want to pause to let things settle down. Get people acclimatised, let the project bed in a little before moving on to the next stage.

- In very big projects involving large scale change, chunk up the work – deliver, pause, embed, check it works, move on to the next bit.

Brown paper planning

- This technique is used by a lot of businesses because it is a simple way to start the planning process.
- It is called 'Brown paper planning' because it is exactly that – it uses a big sheet of brown paper.
- It is a great way to get your team bought into the planning process.

In very simple terms:
- Put a big long sheet of brown paper on the wall and timeline it.
- Write out on post-it notes the work that needs doing.
- Get the team to discuss where to put the post-its on the timeline.
- It generates discussion as to what needs to be done and when.
- It helps make sure you have thought of everything – when you start to prioritise things you very often think of something else that needs doing first.
- The post-its can be moved around until you are happy with your plan.
- It's great a process if you are away off site with your team on (say) a strategy day. The brown paper plan can be rolled up and taken away and put up back in the office.
- The information can then be transferred to your formal project management software.

Measure progress

- This is covered in more detail in Section 5. It is important that you keep on top of your plans.

- Always measure progress towards achieving your targets and objectives.

- Checking progress should be a routine. Put it in the plan.

- Remember to use milestones to check that you are up to where you need to be – as per your plan.

- Continually re-assess whether your plan is realistic and achievable under your timescales.

- Once your plan is underway keep abreast of new data, events, issues etc that affect what you are doing.

- It is okay to re-plan.

- Plan, plan and plan again until you are happy.

- Communicate progress. Communicate, communicate and communicate again until everyone is happy.

The •peoplemad success model

Today
Tomorrow
Execution ✓
Strategy
Goals
Plan

•peoplemad © Phil Merrick

Execute your strategy

Vision

Right objectives
Right actions

Where you are today

Right people

Right jobs

Right environment

Execution

- Execution is about implementing your vision and strategy, putting your plans in place and making things happen.
- This is the essence of •**peoplemad**
    - –Surround yourself with the right people
    - –Get the right people doing the right things
    - –Create the right environment
- Execution will be a combination of carrying out your normal day to day business activity and a series of projects designed to deliver your strategy.
- In simple terms projects differ from business as usual in that they have a start and end date and a specific set of deliverables that need to be completed within those dates.
- Projects impacting the business will need time to bed in – the integration of projects into business activity needs careful thought and planning. Especially the impact on people.
- You want the best people all focused on delivering the strategy, working hard in an environment that allows them to flourish.
- Don't underestimate how hard it is to get this right. Strategy is nothing without effective execution.

Impact on other people

- Whenever you are making decisions and taking action it will invariably affect other people.
- Think about the impact you are having on other people's lives and emotions.
- Remember that you need other people to make things work.
- Think about what you say and how you say it.
- Be honest.
- If you are uncomfortable delivering difficult messages then seek advice, obtain training.
- Giving good messages needs as much preparation and attention as giving difficult messages.
- Always think – 'how will this make people feel?'
- When you communicate with someone always consider 'how do I want them to feel? What do I want them to do about it? It helps you choose the right words.
- Remember people perform better when they feel good about themselves.
- These points hold true for everyday life situations but are magnified in times of change.

The •**peoplemad** success model

Develop your strategy

Today • Tomorrow • Execution • Strategy • Goals • Plan

•peoplemad © Phil Merrick

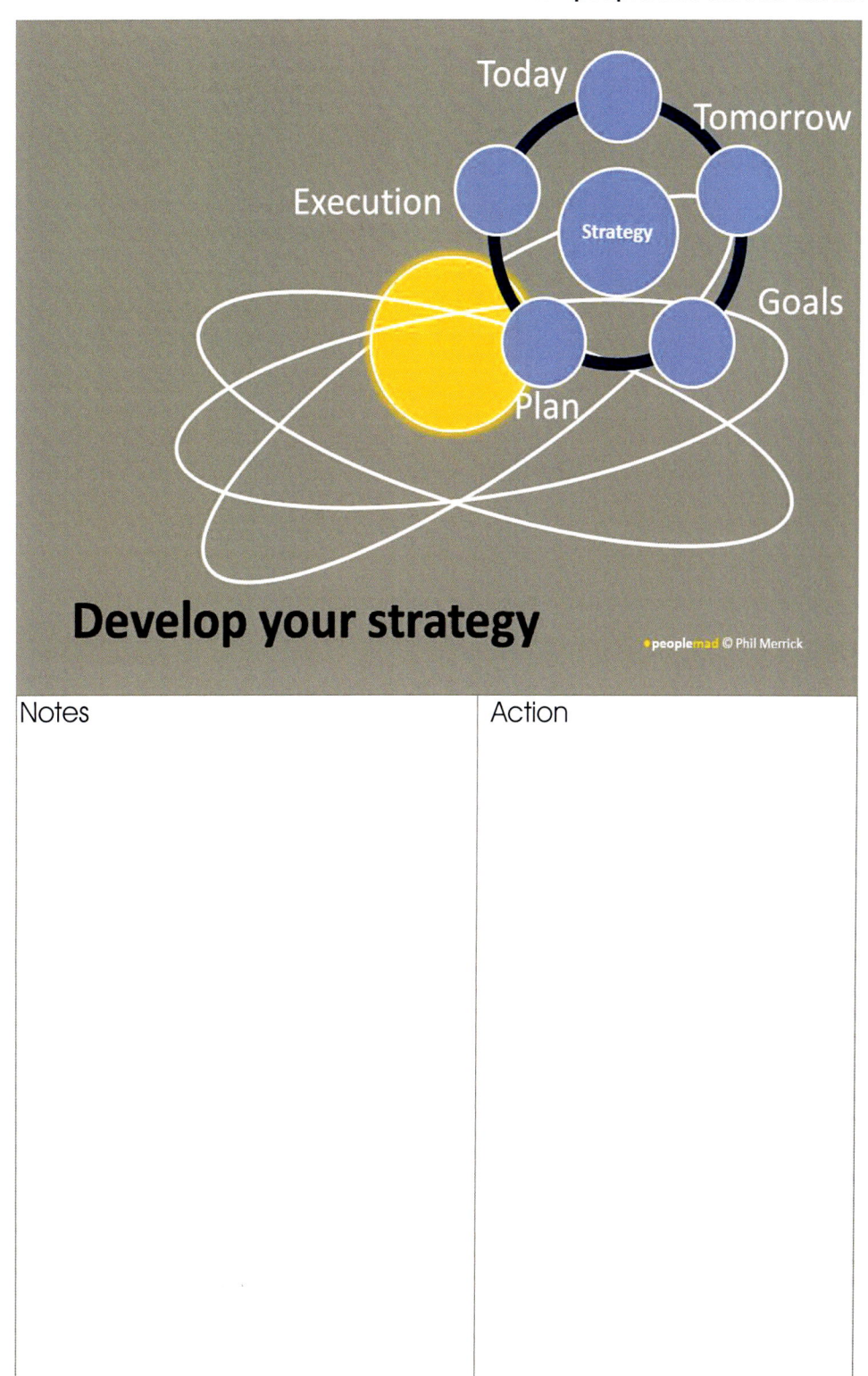

Notes	Action

Your own •**peoplemad** notes

4. Surround yourself with the right people

In this section:
- The •**peoplemad** success model
- The important points up front
- Remember the rule
- Attitude is everything
- Initiative
- Beliefs
- Beliefs: values and morals
- Winning mentality
- Work ethic
- Ability comes from hard work
- Talent
- Skill
- Knowledge
- Experience

'I really do believe that it's about the people that are around you that creates how you see things.'
Judy Murray, mother of tennis player Andy Murray. June 2014.

Surround yourself with the right people continued

In this section continued:
- Common sense
- Potential
- Personality is essential
- Personality
- Sense of humour
- Other people affect your happiness…
- Recruitment
- The recruitment process
- Choosing your leaders
- Choosing your leaders: a word of warning
- Assessment
- Reviewing is a continual process
- Leadership tips
- Your own •**peoplemad** notes

'Surround yourself with good, lucky people, they will make you look amazingly good.'
Allan Leighton, businessman who sold ASDA to US retail giant Wal-Mart.

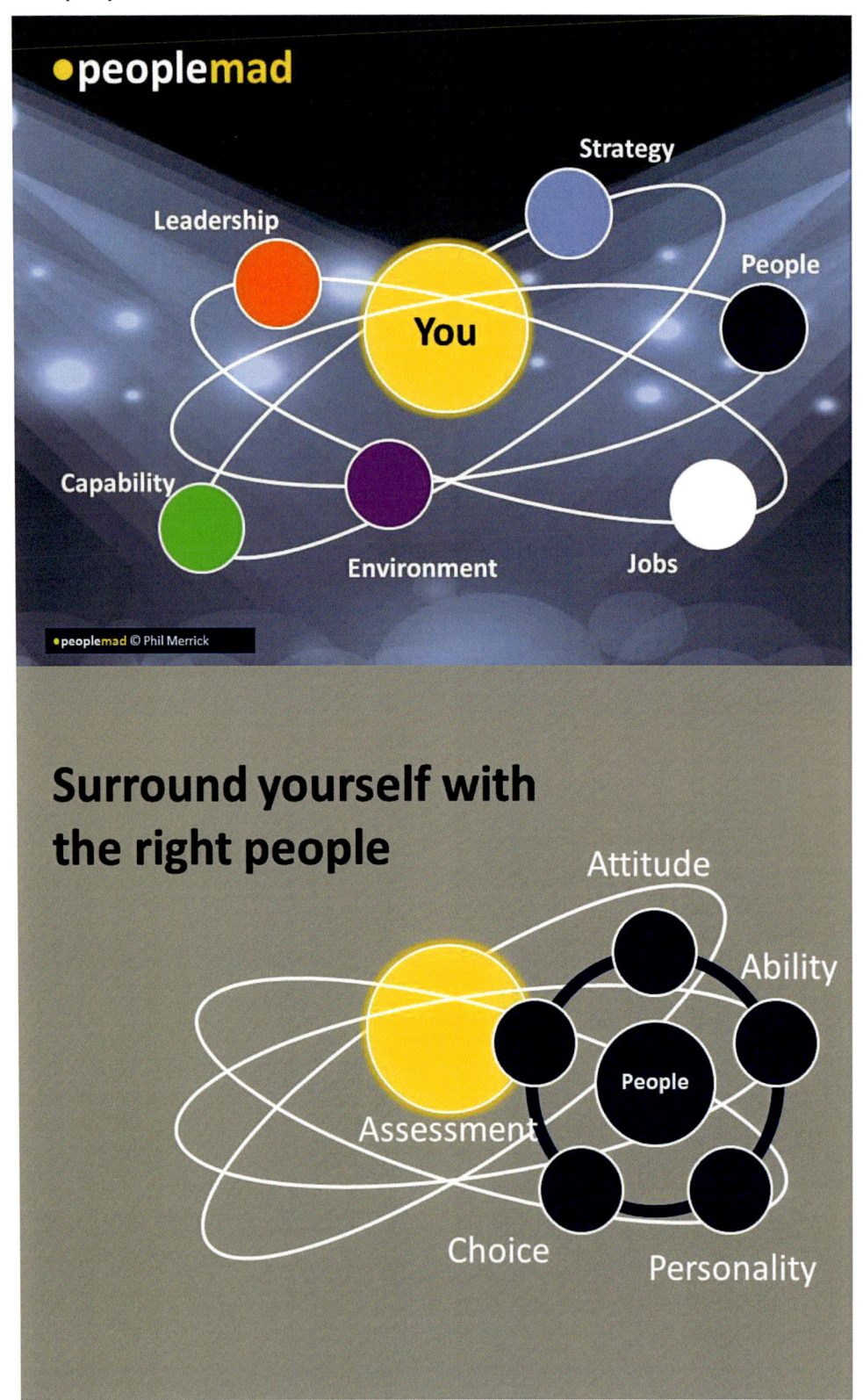

The •peoplemad success model

•peoplemad

Strategy
Leadership
You
People
Capability
Environment
Jobs

•peoplemad © Phil Merrick

Surround yourself with the right people

Attitude
Ability
People
Assessment
Choice
Personality

- The model is called ●**peoplemad** for a reason.
- You are who you mix with. Surround yourself with the right people. – *the* most important statement in this book.
- *In life,* not just in business.
- Life and business is about building relationships and dealing with other people. That's all there is. Just reflect for a second – most of our lives are spent speaking to, listening to or watching other people.
- You don't do business with companies – you do business with the people who work in those companies. The outcome will be determined by your relationship with those people.

Make sure you are good at relationships because *people deal with people they like dealing with.*

In business –
How much time do you spend on people matters?
How much time do you waste on people matters?
There is a huge difference.
How many people do you recruit, train, coach, mentor, appraise, discipline and then eventually have to let go?
Lost man hours, wasted effort, huge costs.
The saying 'get it right first time' has to be applied to recruitment.
Only recruit the right person and – don't 'make do' because there is no-one else. The best of a bad bunch is still bad.

The ●peoplemad success model

And a very important point – you are responsible for the people you recruit. Help them, make sure they are happy in their work, give them the tools to succeed. Take ownership of the people you employ. And think of it this way – if you recruit somebody and then have to fire them it should really hurt you.

You are as much to blame because you decided they were right for the job in the first place.

I'll give you an example:

Football Chairmen – they just don't get this.

By the summer of 2014 new Leeds owner Massimo Cellino had sacked his 36th manager in 22 years at his Italian club Cagliari.

Chelsea had 9 managers in 6 years before reverting back to Jose Mourinho who they let go in 2004.

Spurs manager Tim Sherwood was given an 18 month contract, did a great job and was sacked after 5 months.

Apart from being disruptive and all the other negative elements related to this sort of practice there's also the huge financial cost of terminating contracts. David Moyes sacked by Manchester United after just 10 months is reported to have been paid millions in compensation. The circumstances are different for each club of course but it's usually because the Chairman is desperate to improve results and bows to pressure from the media and importantly the fans.

This emphasises the point that people can be very powerful especially as a group with passion, strong beliefs and a common cause, like their football team.

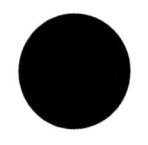

The important points up front

- 'Surround yourself with the right people' is an important rule. Stick to it.
- It applies in every situation – life and business.
- You need people who will help you achieve your objectives and help you live your life as you want it to be.
- It is important that people should complement each other – they don't have to be like each other.
- Ability is important – having the right skills, knowledge and experience.
- Having the right attitude is critical.
- Don't surround yourself with clones of yourself or people who are afraid to challenge what you do and say.
- Always pick the best person for the job, irrespective of creed, gender or race.

'I love argument, I love debate. I don't expect anyone just to sit there and agree with me, that's not their job.'
Margaret Thatcher, British Prime Minister.

The •peoplemad success model

Remember the rule: Surround yourself with the right people

- People are powerful creatures, they:
    - Communicate
    - Create things
    - Have ideas
    - Make decisions
    - Take action
    - Have feelings and emotions
    - Develop technology
    - Influence other people
- Use this power to your advantage - see people as a force.
- It is impossible to be an expert on everything – focus on what you do best and get the help of the experts for everything else.
- Be careful not to prejudge based on first impressions – it's amazing what you can discover and learn from people from all walks of life.
- **The quicker you get the best people on your side the quicker you'll get there.**

'The same man cannot be well skilled in everything; each has his own special excellence.'
Euripedes, Greek tragic dramatist.

The **•peoplemad** success model

People are the most important asset in any organisation and are more important than systems, buildings, processes and even products (because products don't produce themselves). In life we are influenced and impacted by the people with whom we choose to spend our time.

> Just in case you've forgotten
>
> **Surround yourself with the right people**

'You're only as good as your players.'
Neil Lennon, Manager Celtic FC. On being named Scottish Premier League Manager of the Year. May 2012.

The •peoplemad success model

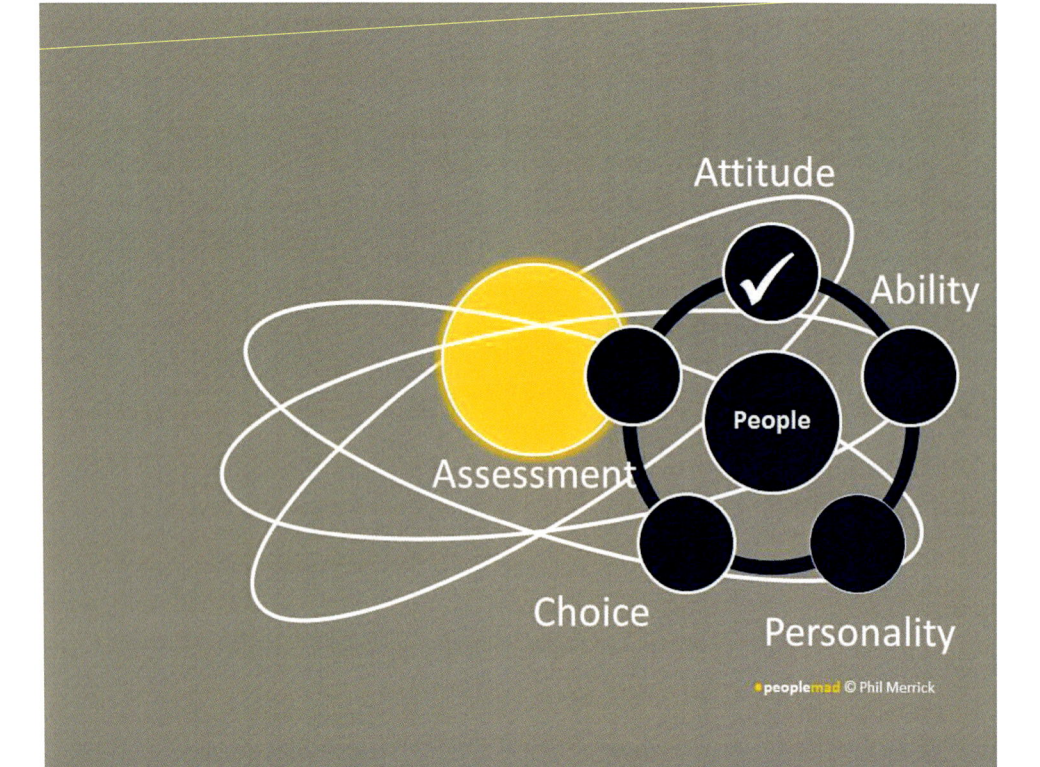

Attitude
Ability
People
Assessment
Choice
Personality

•peoplemad © Phil Merrick

Attitude is everything

100% positive

Beliefs
Initiative
Winning mentality
Work ethic

Attitude is everything. As I said earlier – having the right attitude is a key factor in believing in yourself. There used to be a sign in the corridor in our Training Centre at the Bank of Scotland saying: 'Attitude is infectious is yours worth catching? ' Attitude comes from beliefs. Beliefs stir feelings and emotions and when you feel strongly about something you will behave in a way that reflects those feelings. Religion… feeling wronged… a cause you feel strongly about… your football team. So if you want to change someone's attitude towards something then the only sure fire way of doing it is to try and change their beliefs – which is actually very difficult. If you can get everyone on your side believing in what you're doing then you've cracked it… and it's a great feeling when there's a common goal and every one is excited and enthused by it. Some people will go to extraordinary lengths to support something they believe in. Always look for the right attitude first and foremost when you're recruiting people because you can teach people how to do the job… it's very difficult trying to change someone's attitude.

A word of caution: make sure you can spot the difference between confidence and arrogance. Confidence is good, arrogance is dangerous. To improve performance you have to continually look at what you're doing and see if you can do it better. Arrogant people think they know everything already and are not interested in what other people have to say.
They only look in the mirror to admire themselves, not to question themselves.

The •peoplemad success model

And when we talk about surrounding yourself with the right people, then surround yourself with winners.

Winning people have winning ways – they know what's needed to be a winner.

They inspire other people to be winners, they are positive and they don't think about failure.

They have high energy levels and a desire to get things done.

And they absolutely hate losing – 'show me a good loser and I'll show you a loser'.

Damon Hill, British World Champion motor racing driver said:

'Winning is everything. The only ones who remember you when you come second are your wife and your dog.'

'I am an optimist. It does not seem too much use being anything else.' **Sir Winston Churchill, British Prime Minister.**

'Attitude is everything.'
Phil Merrick.

The •**peoplemad** success model

●

Attitude plays an important part in building personal capability in Section 7.
This is the differentiator between success and failure.

'People are always blaming their circumstances for what they are. I don't believe in circumstances. The people who get on in this World are the people who get up and look for the circumstances they want, and, if they can't find them, make them.'
George Bernard Shaw, Irish dramatist and critic.

'You can do anything if you have enthusiasm. Enthusiasm is the yeast that makes your hopes rise to the stars. Enthusiasm is the spark in your eye, the swing in your gait, the grip of your hand, the irresistible surge of your will and energy to execute your ideas... Enthusiasm is at the bottom of all progress!'
Henry Ford, American motor manufacturer.

Initiative

- The Oxford English Dictionary definition is: **The ability to initiate or begin something;** On one's own initiative: **without being prompted by others.**

- People with initiative:
    - Have 'get up and go'
    - Think for themselves
    - Don't wait to be told what to do
- Initiative stems from inherent enthusiasm.
- People with initiative don't need pushing – they need guiding and controlling.
- Initiative comes from a desire to take action.
- Initiative is a great quality in someone - don't stifle it with too many procedures and rules.
- Encourage, praise, and monitor.*
- Caution* there is a risk that people with initiative do the wrong things if they don't wait to be told what to do.

'There are three types of people: Those who make things happen, those who watch things happen and those who ask 'what happened?' **Anon.**

Beliefs

- The Oxford English Dictionary definition is: ***A firmly held opinion or conviction.***

- If you feel strongly about something you will behave in a way that reflects those feelings (religion, a cause, feeling wronged).
- This is because your beliefs determine your attitude towards something which then drives your behaviour.
- A simple example:
    - Belief: the manager of your football team is not good enough
    - Attitude: you have lost all faith and want him out
    - Behaviour: you join in protest marches and chant anti manager songs during the match.
- It follows that in order to change someone's behaviour then the best way to do it would be to change their beliefs.
- This is a powerful subject and plays a big part in improving personal performance – see Section 7.

'I do the very best I know how – the very best I can; and I mean to keep doing it until the end.' **Abraham Lincoln, President of the United States of America.**

The ●peoplemad success model

Beliefs: values and morals

- **The Oxford English Dictionary definition:**
    - **–Values:** principles or standards of behaviour.
- **The Oxford English Dictionary definition:**
    - **–Morals:** principles of right or wrong.

- Values and morals are beliefs about behaviour and what you perceive to be the difference between right and wrong. They are put together here because they both determine attitude.
- Attitude drives behaviour – people feel strongly about their values and morals and are rarely prepared to change – which means the same behaviours will continue.
- If your team has shared values and an agreed code of behaviour then they are more likely to gel and get on with each other.
- Trust comes from an understanding of each others values.
- Don't try to inflict your beliefs on other people – they have as much right to their beliefs as you have to yours.

'Nothing great was ever achieved without enthusiasm.'
Ralph Waldo Emerson, American poet, essayist and philosopher.

The ●peoplemad success model

Disciplining yourself to do what you know is right and important, although difficult, is the highroad to pride, self-esteem, and personal satisfaction.'
Margaret Thatcher, British Prime Minister.

'Don't compromise yourself. You are all you've got.'
Janis Joplin, American singer.

'Integrity is the essence of everything successful.'
R. Buckminster Fuller, American author and inventor.

'We wanted to act with integrity. We were not going to get pretentious or try to humiliate the opposition by showboating or trying to nutmeg everybody or whatever nonsense.'
Thomas Muller, German footballer after beating Brazil 7-1 in the World Cup Finals July 2014.

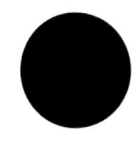

Winning mentality

- The Oxford English Dictionary definition is:
  –Winner: a person or thing that wins.
  –Mentality: characteristic way of thinking.

- Winning people have winning ways – they know what's needed to be a winner.
- Winners inspire other people to be winners.
- Winners are positive people – they don't think about failure.
- Winners usually have high energy levels and a desire to get things done.
- Winners who have tasted success want more of it.
- Winners hate losing – 'show me a good loser and I'll show you a loser'.
- Be a winner, surround yourself with winners.

'Winners are winners before they win'.
Jessie Jay, English singer and song-writer.

Work ethic

- The Oxford English Dictionary definition is:
    - *Work: activity involving mental or physical effort done in order to achieve a result*
    - *Ethic: set of moral principles.*
- People with a strong work ethic believe that working hard is the right thing to do – it is one of their values.
- Talent alone is not enough - success needs hard work.
- Skills have to be learnt – they only improve with practise, practise and more practise.
- Successful people are not afraid of hard work.
- The 'work smarter not harder' saying should be 'work smarter and harder'.
- Make hard work a value for you and your team.
- Find a job you enjoy doing and it won't seem like hard work.
- Caution 'All work no play' is dangerous. It is important for people to find the right 'work/life balance' that works for their own personal circumstances (see Section 7 Work hard, play hard).

'Work is much more fun than fun.'
Sir Noel Coward, English actor and dramatist.

The •peoplemad success model

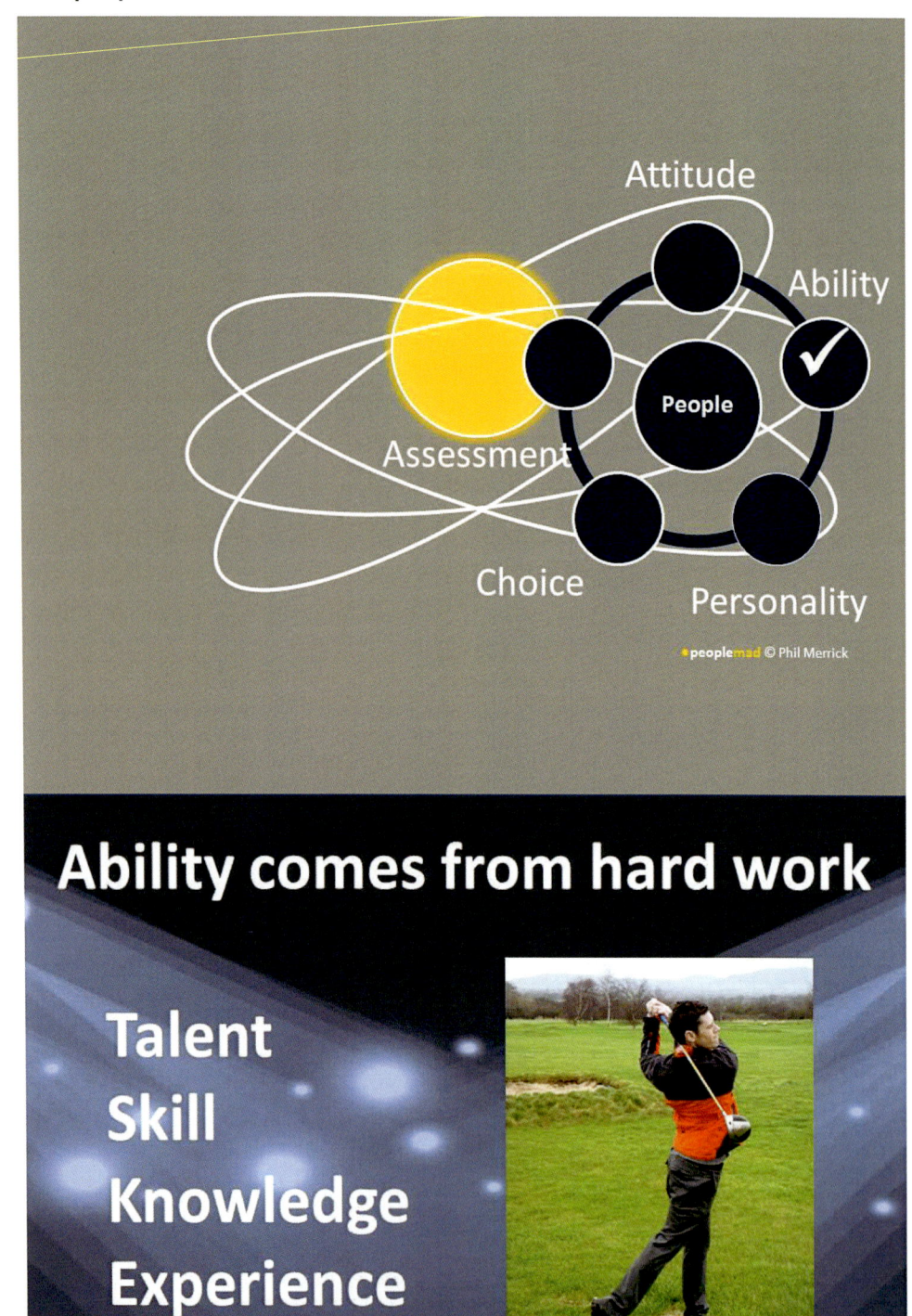

Attitude
Ability
People
Assessment
Choice
Personality

•peoplemad © Phil Merrick

Ability comes from hard work

Talent
Skill
Knowledge
Experience

The •peoplemad success model

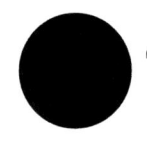

● **'There are no short cuts, just hard work'.** Mo Farah, 2012 and 2016 Double Olympic Gold Medallist.

It goes without saying that successful people need ability and having the right skills, knowledge and experience to do the job is an absolute must.

The better other people are at doing their jobs the better your life will be – especially in a team situation.

If you are the manager **you'll** be judged on how well your team performs.

Also make sure you use people to their full potential. If you don't get the best out of someone and don't use all their skills to best effect then you're losing out; in income terms because you're not fully utilising what's at your disposal, or in cost terms because your costs are higher than they need to be. It's a waste of valuable resource and it's not fair on the person; high achievers want to be stretched and challenged.

'I don't know anything about luck. I've never banked on it, and I'm afraid of people who do. Luck to me is something else: hard work and realising what is opportunity and what isn't.'
Lucille Ball, American actress.

The •peoplemad success model

Talent

- The Oxford English Dictionary definition is: **Natural aptitude or skill.**
- Some people are naturally gifted at doing certain things.
- It is no coincidence that talented children often have talented parents but it is not necessarily about their DNA.
- Starting at an early age, having purpose, hours of practise, best tutorship and a belief in your own ability all foster this 'natural' aptitude.
- Whether talent is a gift or something that is learned, it still needs to be nurtured and developed.
- You will have talents that other people don't have – use them to your advantage.
- Other people have talents that you don't have – use them to your advantage
- Talent is wasted if it is not married with the right attitude and application.

' We work really hard to make it look easy .'
Mo Martin, USA Ladies professional golfer. July 2016.

Skill

The Oxford English Dictionary definition is: ***The ability to do something well.***

You will be good at something if you:
- Have the best coach/teacher
- Learn the right technique
- Work hard
- Believe in yourself
- Yearn to be the best you can
- Practise, practise, practise
- Don't give up.

- Watch other people who already have that skill.
- Give yourself the advantage - be able to do something better than everybody else.
- ***Dealing effectively with other people is a skill.*** Make this skill important to you.
- Work at it, practise, practise, practise.

Getting results through people is a skill that cannot be learned in the classroom.'
Jean Paul Getty, American financier.

Knowledge

- The Oxford English Dictionary definition is: ***Information and skills acquired through experience and education.***

- Make sure you have the right knowledge aligned to achieving your objectives.
- Do things.
- Read things.
- Learn things.
- Write things down.
- Get interested in different things.
- Ask questions.
- Be more interested in other people than you are in yourself.

- The more knowledge you have the more you will be able to apply common sense to decision making. This saves time and is key to improving performance.

'The more extensive a man's knowledge of what has been done, the greater will be his power of knowing what to do.'
Benjamin Disraeli, British Prime Minister and Statesman.

The ●peoplemad success model

Experience

- The Oxford English Dictionary definition is: **Practical contact with and observation of facts or events.**

- This should be broader than just having experience in the job in hand.
- The more you do, the better informed you will be.
- The better informed you are then the easier it will be to make the right decisions.
- Experience in subjects unrelated to your objectives is still important experience.
- Experience doesn't come from age, it comes from doing things.
- Get out there and do things – including travel (not just abroad) to see different people and cultures.
- Get as much experience of dealing with people as you can possibly get.
- Read more, ask more questions.
- Get interested in other people.

'Progress comes from the intelligent use of experience.'
Elbert Hubbard, American businessman, writer.

Common sense

- The Oxford English Dictionary definition is: **Good sense and sound judgement in practical matters.**

- Common sense can be considered to be an essential skill and will be continually improved through knowledge and experience.
- Success is about making the right decisions more often than you make the wrong ones – this requires sound judgement.
- A practical approach helps to 'keep things simple' – a requirement of **•peoplemad**.
- Common sense is the ability to think rationally which helps in pressure situations and when decisions are needed to be made quickly.
- Taking a 'common sense' approach to most things can save time and energy – eliminating the need for in depth research and analysis.
- Your gut feel is usually right – check it out, test it, learn to use it.
- Practise, practise, practise.

- Note: Think carefully about the impact before changing a decision. Changing your mind for the right reason is obviously okay but can be disruptive and hinder progress especially if people have already started to take action.

Common sense

'If it looks like a duck, and quacks like a duck, then it is 95 per cent certain it is a duck. You don't have to send it away for DNA testing to prove it is a duck, because by the time you get to prove it is a duck, it has flown away.'
Stuart Rose, CEO Marks & Spencer.

'Self belief is the key to driving performance and getting results. It is easy to believe in yourself when results are good. When things aren't going so well it is the self belief that will help get things back on track. Keep the belief.'
Phil Merrick.

'I've not failed. I've just found 10,000 ways that won't work'.
Thomas Edison, American inventor.

The •peoplemad success model

Potential

- The Oxford English Dictionary definition is: ***Having the capacity to develop into something in the future.***
- Developing potential is rewarding and helps to improve team performance as people continually improve their own individual performances. It helps with camaraderie and team bonding. The alternative is to replace them with somebody better, which could be beneficial but can also be disruptive and costly.
- Everyone has potential, not everyone has drive
    - –Can they improve?
    - –Do they want to improve?
    - –Are they prepared to work at it?
    - –How good can they get?
    - –Can you afford to wait?
- Get good at spotting the people with potential.
- Get good at spotting the people with potential **and the right attitude.**

'Seven of those Barcelona players tonight came through the ranks of their club and that helps to make them an unstoppable force.'
Gary Neville, Manchester United and England International player and coach.

The •peoplemad success model

Diagram: atomic/orbital model with central "People" circle surrounded by Attitude, Ability, Personality (✓), Choice, and Assessment (yellow).

•peoplemad © Phil Merrick

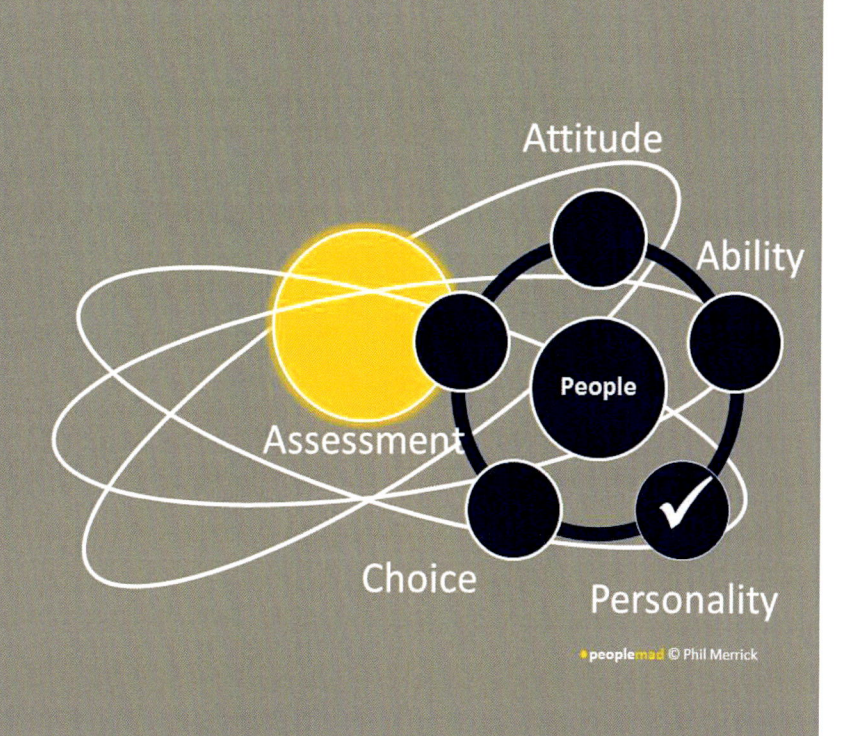

Personality is essential

Cartoon: a man writing "PERSONALITY?" on a board.

People deal with people they like dealing with

Personality

- The Oxford English Dictionary definition is: ***The combination of characteristics or qualities that form an individual's distinctive character – lively, engaging qualities.***

- People deal with people – you want your people to be able to engage confidently with other people.
- Can they make eye contact?
- Are they comfortable making conversation?
- Are they interested in other people?
- Do they smile?
- You can often read a person by their eyes.
- Do you like the person? If you don't there is a good chance other people won't either.
- Learn to read body language.
- Get good at reading people.
- Listen to what they mean not necessarily to what they say.

'People deal with people they like dealing with.'
Phil Merrick.

Sense of humour

- The Oxford English Dictionary definition is: **The ability to appreciate or express humour.**

- Laughter is an enjoyable experience – it raises spirits and makes people feel good about themselves.
- Being able to laugh at things releases tension.
- Humour is a big part of team camaraderie.
- **CAUTION:**
    - Team camaraderie often involves 'mickey taking' – there is a limit to what is acceptable and must not be cruel and divisive.
    - Work must be taken seriously and humour must not detract from the job at hand.
    - Always respect your colleagues, their workloads and their personal circumstances.
- You need to be able to laugh at yourself- it helps with team spirit.
- Work hard, play hard, have fun.

'If you want people to be glad to meet you, you must be glad to meet them – and show it.'
Johann von Goethe, German poet and writer.

The •**peoplemad** success model

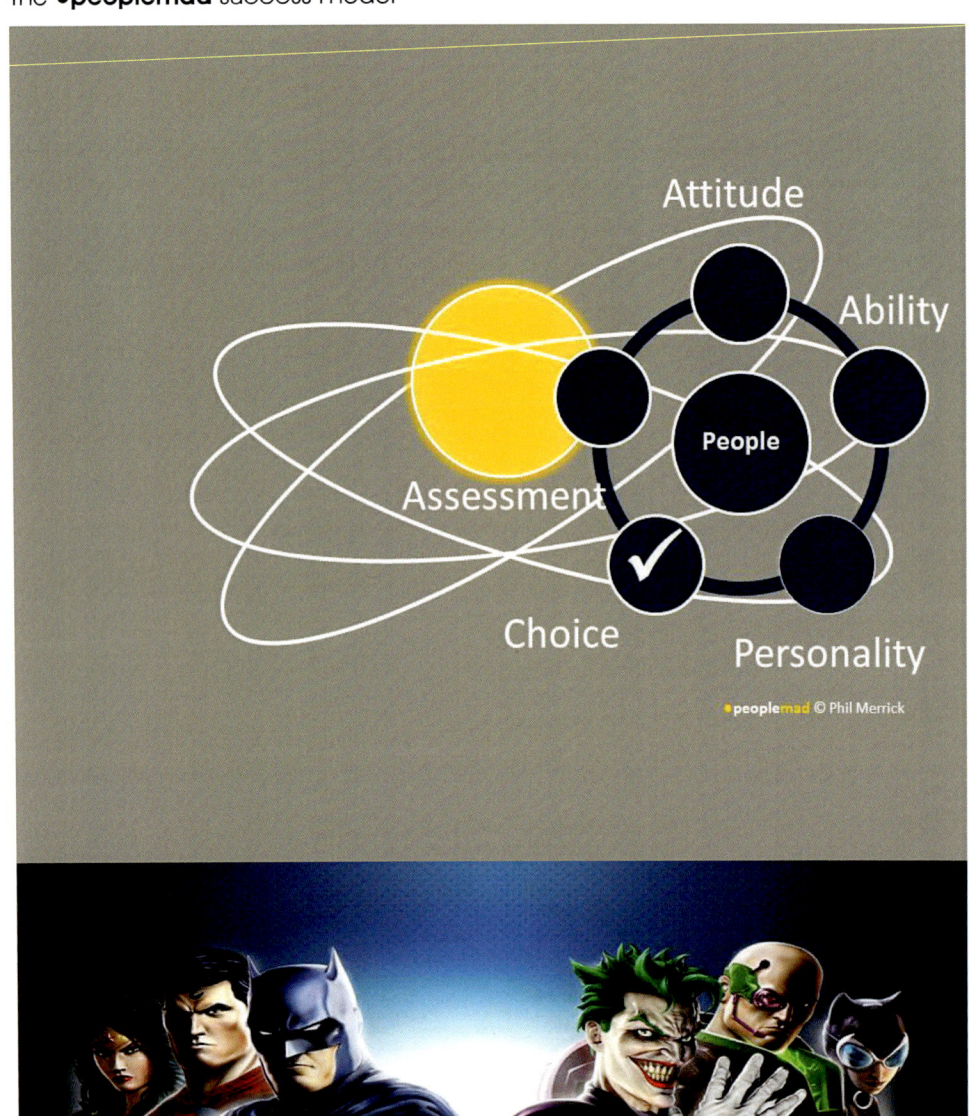

Attitude
Ability
People
Assessment
Choice
Personality

•**peoplemad** © Phil Merrick

Other people affect your happiness and success

Choose them wisely

The •peoplemad success model

Recruitment

Think OUTCOME

- How much time do you spend on people matters?
- How much time do you waste on people matters?
- Do you know the difference?
- If you don't know the answers you should.
- How many people are recruited, trained, coached, mentored, appraised, disciplined and then eventually leave? Lost man hours, wasted effort, huge costs.
- 'Get it right first time' needs to be applied to recruitment.
- To get it right first time choose people with the right:
    - Attitude (more important than capability)
    - Personality (they need to interact with other people)
    - Capability (skills, experience and knowledge)
    - Potential (you will need to invest in development and be prepared to wait for performance to improve over time).

'The best executive is the one who has sense enough to pick good men to do what he wants done, and self restraint enough to keep from meddling with them while they do it.'
Theodore Roosevelt, American President.

The ●peoplemad success model

The recruitment process

Think OUTCOME

- Entice the best people to apply and pick from a big pool.
- Only recruit the right person to the role.
- Don't 'make do' because there is no-one else. The best of a bad bunch is still bad.
- Remember people have potential and will develop with the right encouragement and development.
- You are responsible for the welfare of the people you recruit – help them, make sure they are happy in their work, give them the tools to succeed.
- Take ownership – you are responsible for the performance of the people you employ. If it doesn't work out you are responsible.
- Beware of arrogant people because by their very nature they don't look at themselves to see if they can improve.
- Don't confuse arrogance with confidence which is an attribute.
- **Spotting the right people is a skill – get good at it.**

'As a manager you are responsible for the performance of your people. Take ownership and be accountable. Help, support, nurture, coach, LEAD.'
Phil Merrick.

Choosing your leaders

- Choosing the right manager/captain/supervisor is a critical part of helping a team deliver the right results.
- They must have the right attitude and ability.
- They must display leadership skills.
- They must be good with people.
- They represent you.
- You need someone you can trust.
- This is a form of delegation:
    - Be clear about your expectations
    - Discuss your strategy, plans and tactics
- You can delegate responsibility for managing/captaining/supervising the team but you must remain accountable.
- Stay interested, monitor progress.
- Continually give feedback on how well it is being done.
- Being in charge of other people can be an effective part of someone's development programme.
- Offer help and advice where needed but allow people the chance to show what they can do for themselves.
- Don't stifle them, support them with an open hand.

Choosing your leaders: a word of warning

- Make sure they are available when you need them
    - Try to match the working hours of your manager to those of the team.
    - Managing people is time consuming. They must be able to do their own job effectively and find the time to manage their team.

- Choose someone who is physically located in the right area
    - Managing a team remotely from a different geographical location is not as effective as it would be if you were working alongside your team.
    - In sport your captain needs to play in a position where he/she can affect results.

- Don't reward good performances by making people managers/captains/supervisors
    - Your leaders should be chosen because they are capable of being good leaders.

'Without initiative, leaders are simply workers in Leadership positions.'
Bo Bennett, author and politician.

The ●peoplemad success model

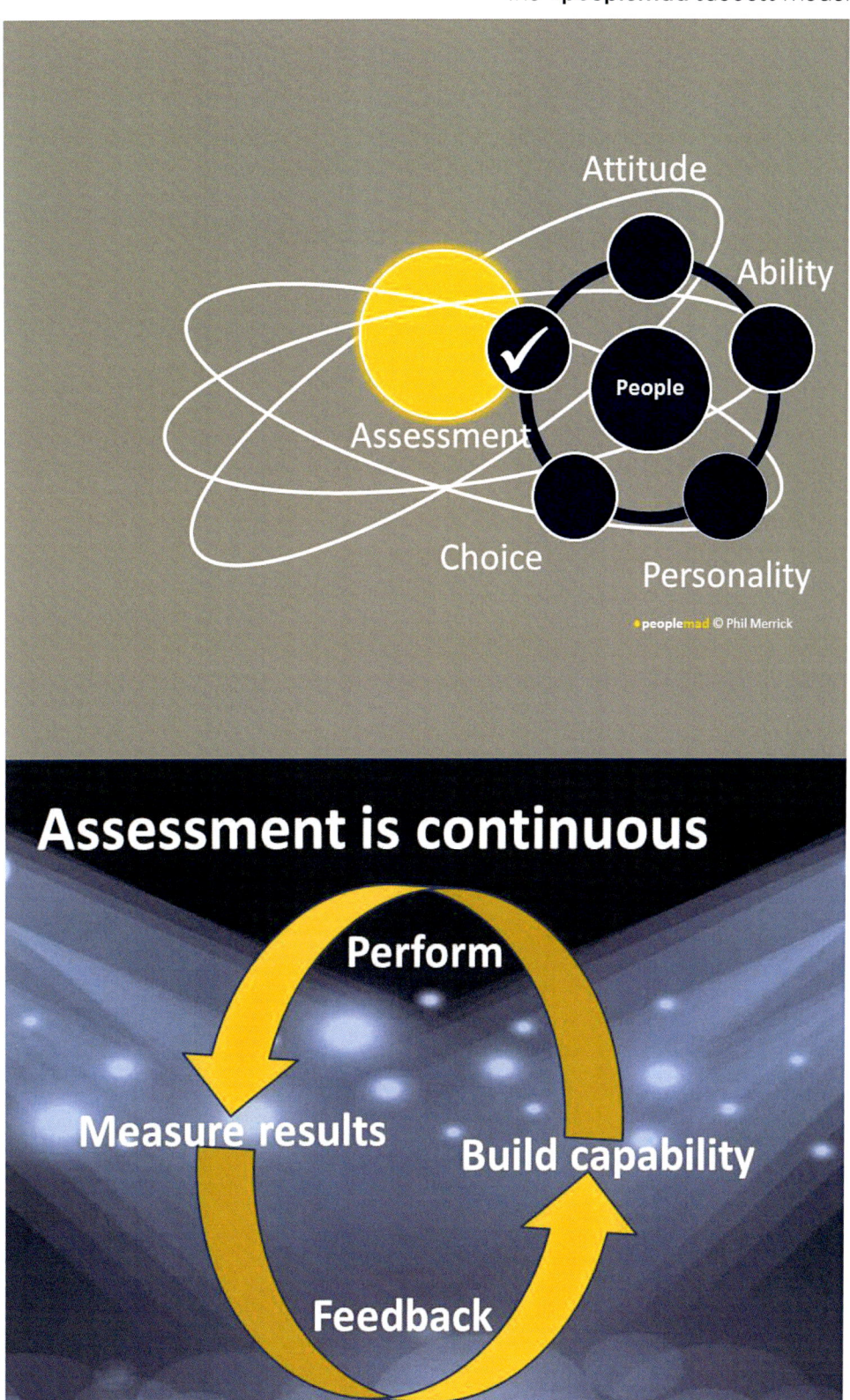

Attitude
Ability
Assessment ✓
People
Choice
Personality

●peoplemad © Phil Merrick

Assessment is continuous

Perform
Build capability
Feedback
Measure results

The •peoplemad success model

Reviewing is a continuous process

Think OUTCOME

- Give support to those who might be experiencing difficulty. Encourage. Have patience.
- Be careful about being dismissive of people who can't improve any further – they are actually performing at their peak and may still be invaluable to your team.
- Be careful not to promote for the wrong reasons – e.g. good sales people don't necessarily make good sales managers. You will lose a good sales person and gain a bad manager. Likewise good footballers don't always make good managers – the roles have an entirely different set of skills.
- Try and get the right blend of youth, experience and talent across the team. Develop from within and supplement with experience brought in from outside.
- See Sections 5 & 9 for notes on how to manage performance.

'The basic difference between being assertive and being aggressive is how our words and behaviour affect the rights and well being of others.'
Sharon Anthony Bower, American writer.

Leadership tips

- Treat everyone the same: with empathy, respect, dignity.
- Good people are hard to find – look after them.
- Continually improve the quality of your people:
    - Planned growth through learning and development
    - The introduction of new people who can meet the required standard or have the potential to do so.
- Succession planning is critical – when people leave it is disruptive. When somebody good leaves there is a risk that performance will be adversely affected, even if it's only temporary.
- Listen closely to what people talk about and how it's said – it's a clue to their personality
    - Do they talk about themselves or other people?
    - Do they dwell on issues or are they generally upbeat?
    - Are they talking at you or are they engaging you?
    - Do they have a purpose to the conversation or are they rambling?
- Watch out for big egos – there's no place for them.
- Take action immediately if you have the wrong people.

The •peoplemad success model

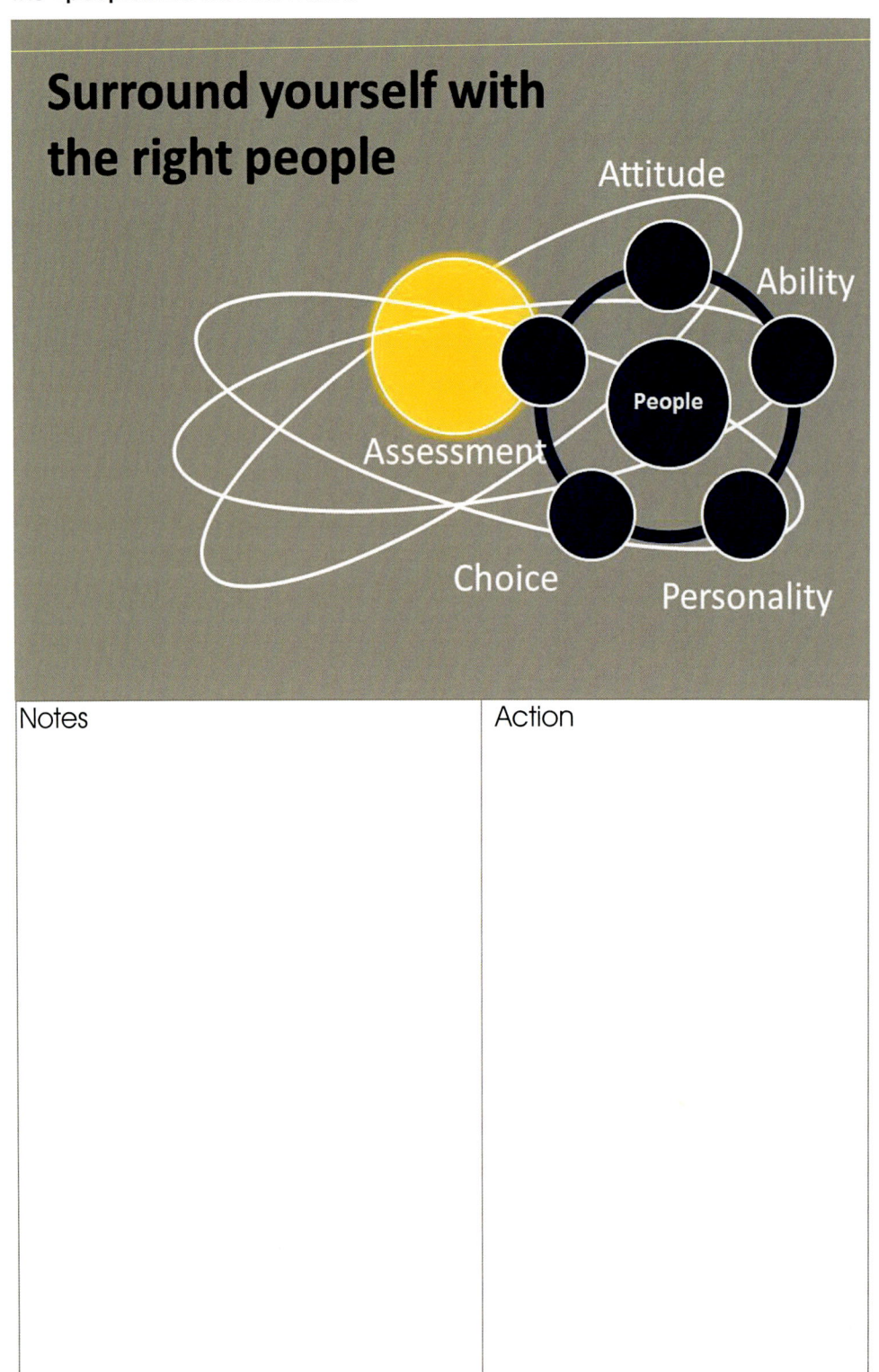

Surround yourself with the right people

- Attitude
- Ability
- People
- Assessment
- Choice
- Personality

Notes	Action

Your own •peoplemad notes

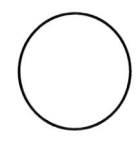

5. Get the right people doing the right things

In this section:

- The •**peoplemad** success model
- Everyone working to a common goal
- Define the work
- Be clear what you expect
- Every activity should be focused on the big picture
- Improving together
- Focus on the right things
- Commitment: get people bought into the vision
- Teach your strategy and approach
- Knowing where you want to be tomorrow
- Align personal and business objectives
- Personal plans should be aligned to business plans
- The principles of good planning
- Role Definition
- Procedures
- Success comes from working hard
- Contribution
- Contribution: Performance Management
- Tools

The •peoplemad success model

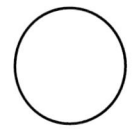

Get the right people doing the right things continued

In this section continued:
- Training
- Training: practise
- Teams: the power of many…
- Teamwork
- Define your team(s)
- Teamwork: delegation
- Trying to fit everyone in
- A football analogy: using good players to 'fill-in'
- Know how well you are doing
- Measurement: Key Performance Indicators
- Measurement: achievement of objectives
- Objectives: setting targets
- High level financial planning
- High level financial monitoring
- Reward the right behaviours
- Recognition
- Risks
- Leadership tips
- Your own •peoplemad notes

The •peoplemad success model

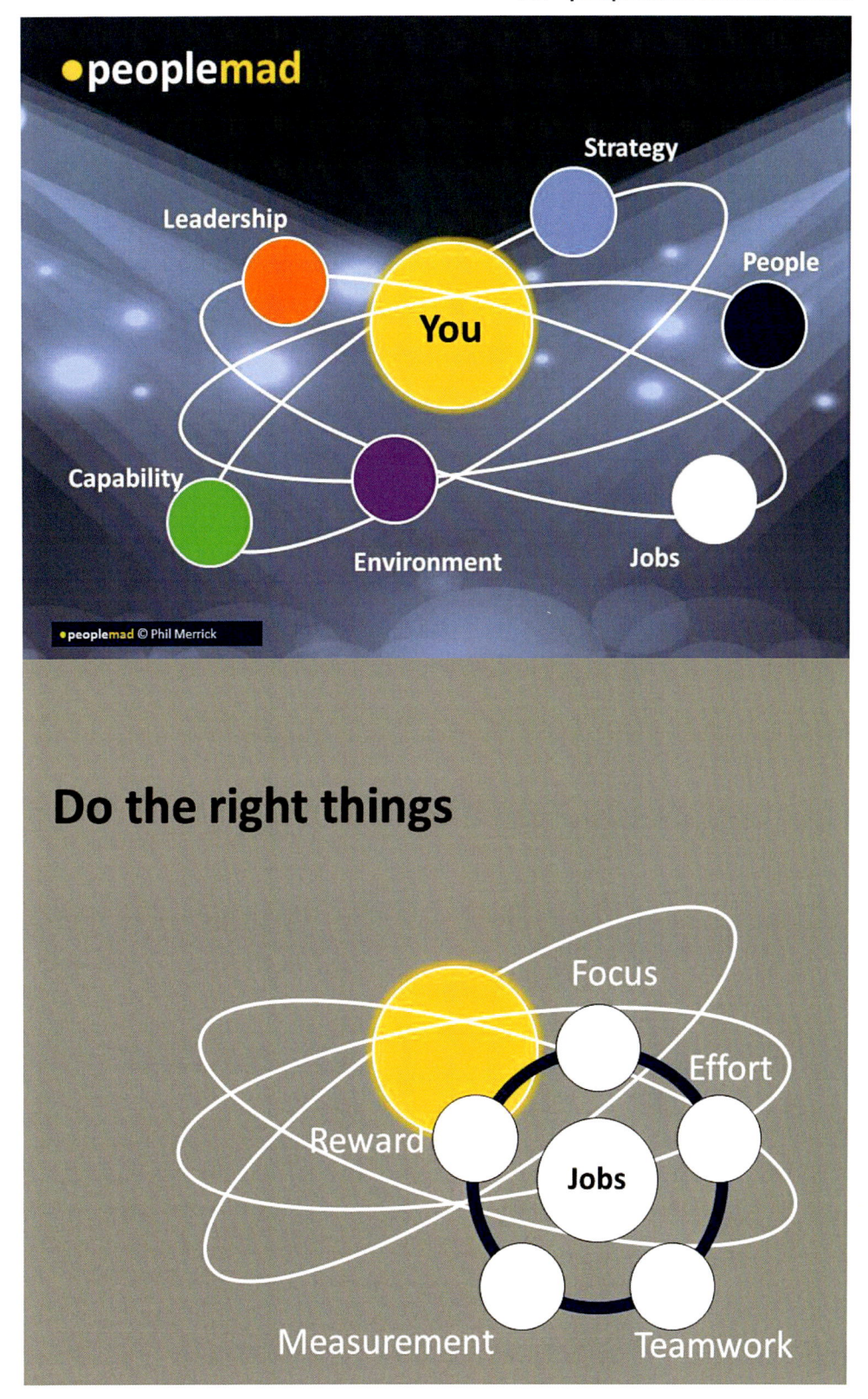

•peoplemad

Leadership · Strategy · You · People · Capability · Environment · Jobs

•peoplemad © Phil Merrick

Do the right things

Focus · Effort · Reward · Jobs · Measurement · Teamwork

The •peoplemad success model

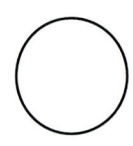

Everyone working to a common goal

Think OUTCOME

- Imagine your team building a house: everyone focused on the one vision. They all have different jobs and a range of different skills needed to make it happen – importantly there's a common goal.
- They all do their best and depending on their experience and training each person does it differently – different speeds, different quality and different results. All the effort goes into achieving the one overall objective – building the house.
- If one piece of the jigsaw isn't done properly it affects everyone else. It needs co-operation, planning and commitment.
- The 3 variables that we talk about in project management are quality, cost and time – if one of these changes it impacts on at least one of the others.
- Applying this metaphor to a huge corporation is far more challenging of course.
- Keep it simple – where the objectives are many or not so readily defined then it is difficult to focus energy on doing the right things.

Business is like riding a bicycle. Either you keep moving or you fall down.'
John David Wright, American businessman.

The •peoplemad success model

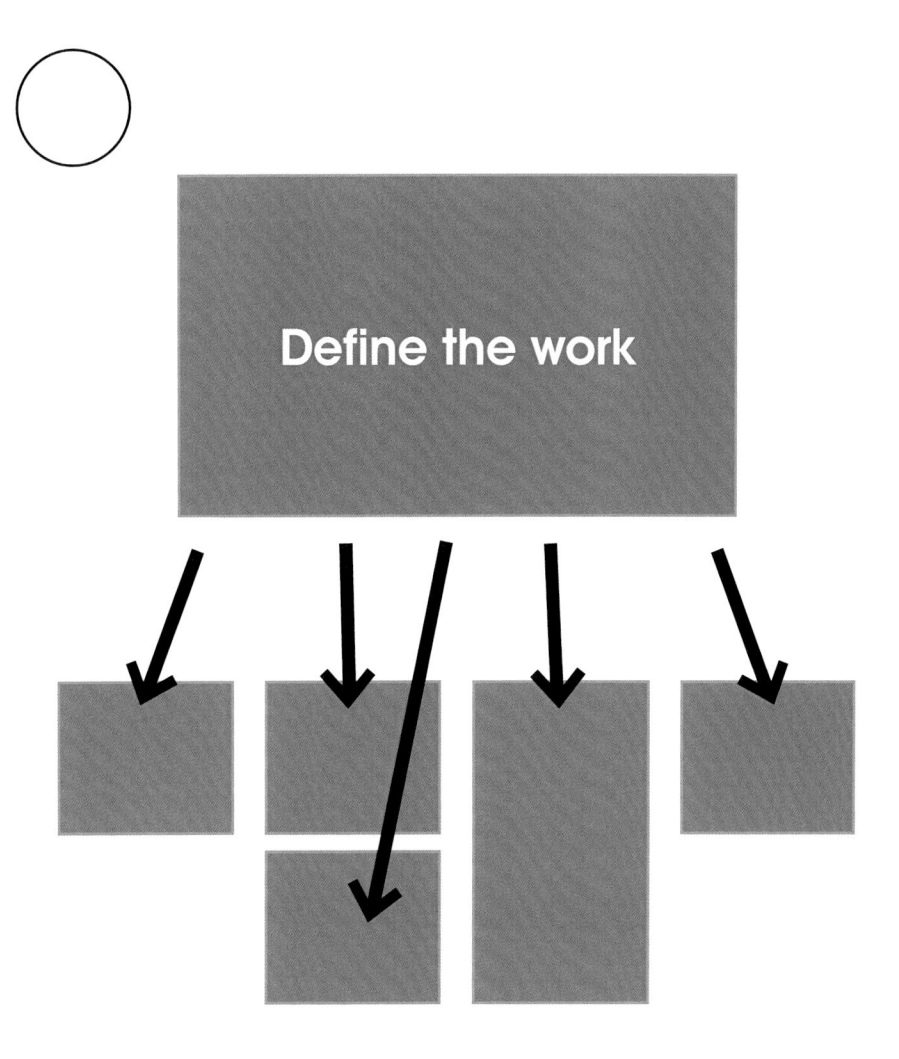

Define the work

Break it down into jobs according to tasks that can be grouped together.

Allocate the jobs to the right people

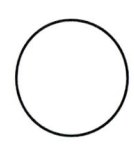

Be clear what you expect

Think OUTCOME

- Peoples' roles need to be clear and well defined.

- When you're defining and planning work be absolutely clear what you want from people.
    - What needs to be done?
    - How will it be done?
    - How well will it be done?
    - Where will it be done?
    - By when will it be finished?
    - Leave no room for doubt.

- Keep it simple – the more straight forward the goals the easier it will be to get people focused on achieving them.

- People like clarity – being clear about responsibilities and what's expected from them really helps from a leadership perspective.

- It helps make people feel good about themselves and people perform better when they feel good about themselves.

The •peoplemad success model

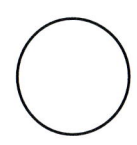

Every activity should be focused on the big picture

Think OUTCOME

- Everything that your people do should lead towards the achievement of your overall vision.
- In theory nothing should be done unless it goes towards building that house.
- Keep it simple – the more straight forward the goal the easier it will be to get people focused on achieving it.

Can you answer these questions about your team or business?

- How much effort is wasted on non productive activity?
- How much time is lost through staff sickness and holidays?
- How much time is wasted on rework – things that need to be done again?
- How much time is lost through people not performing at their best?
- How much time is lost on ineffective training ?
- Wouldn't it be great if 100% effort was performed at 100% quality for 100% of the time? How much more successful would you be?

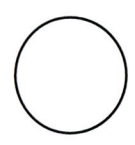

The •**peoplemad** success model

Think
OUTCOME

Ideally…
Everyone should improve together
with the same vision, strategy and
objectives.

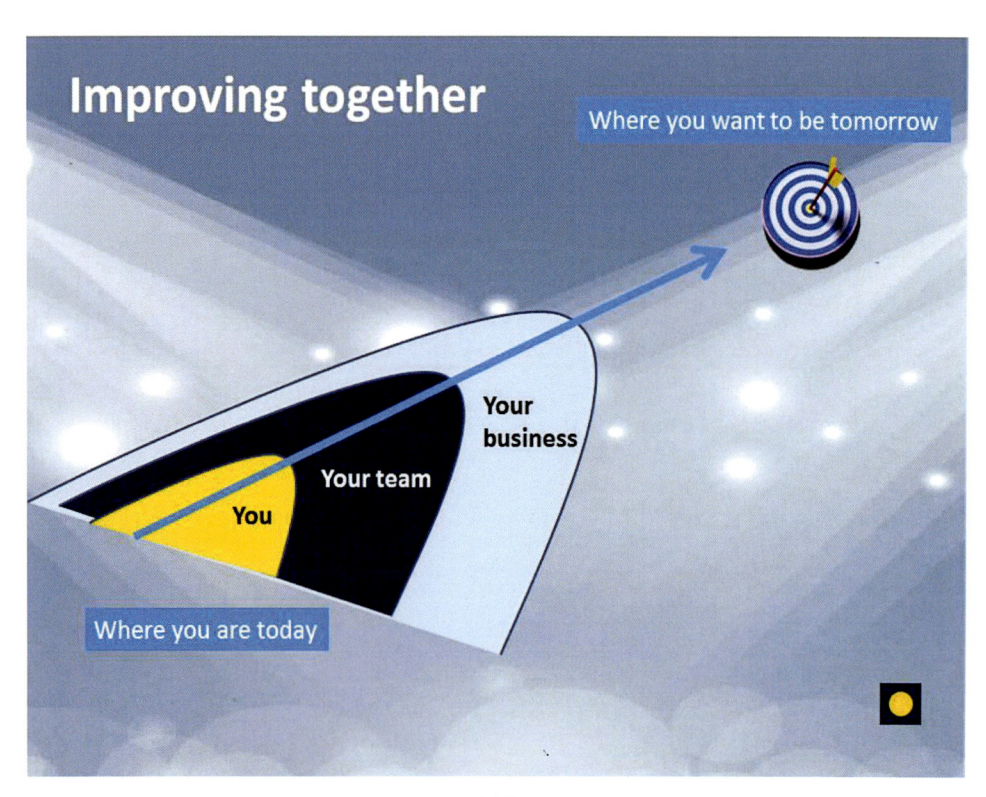

Improving together

Where you want to be tomorrow

Your business
Your team
You

Where you are today

The •peoplemad success model

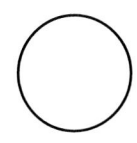

Is everyone in your team performing at their best? Dedicated, focused, happy, determined – delivering?

How much time do you waste on things that slow you down, get in your way, stop you getting to where you want to be?

'We say all the time control the controllables and if you can focus and be the best that you can be at what you can control you give yourself an opportunity. If you start to cloud your mind with things which are beyond your control then you clog your mind up with things that can affect what you can control.'
Nigel Adkins Manager of Southampton FC before being promoted to the Premiership. April 2012.

'There is a better way to do it; find it.'
Thomas A Edison, American inventor.

The •peoplemad success model

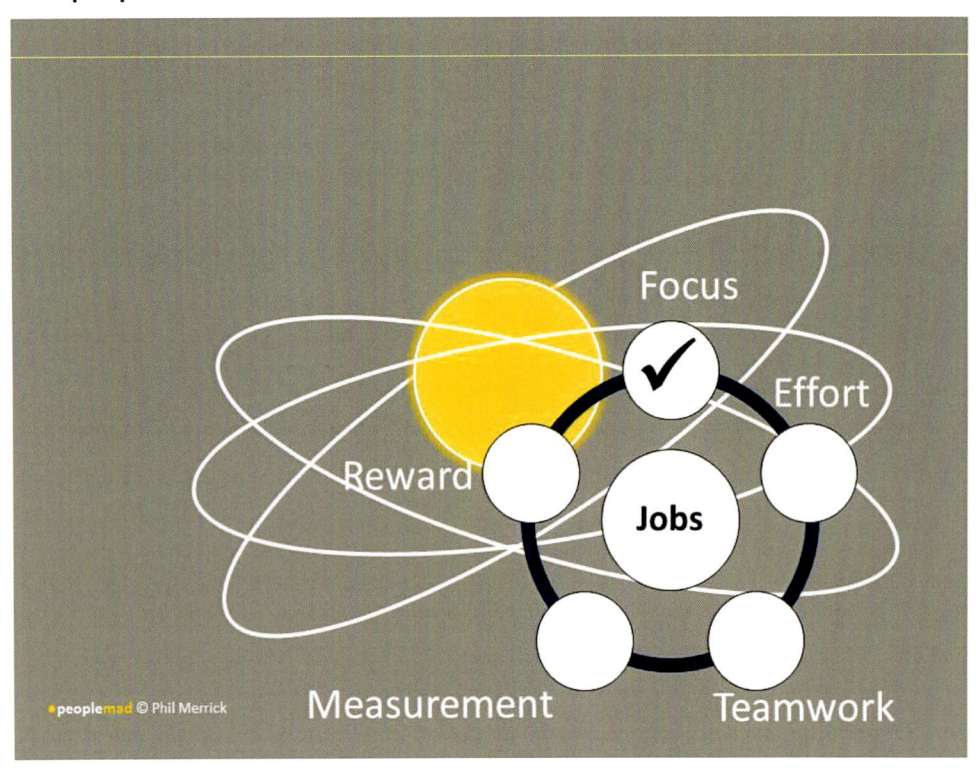

Focus
Effort
Reward
Jobs
Measurement
Teamwork

•peoplemad © Phil Merrick

Vision
Right objectives
Right actions
Where you are today

Focus on the right things

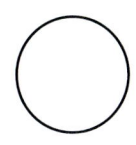

Commitment: get people bought into the vision

Think OUTCOME

- If people share the exact same dream then you have a very powerful team.
- If they are new and were not part of the visioning then sit down with them, get them to understand, get them to want it as much as you.
- Explain the benefits.
- They need to have an emotional attachment; they need to care about what happens.
- Your people must:
    - Aspire, desire, dream.
    - Believe they can do anything that's physically possible.
    - Picture it in their heads.
    - Close their eyes and paint it in their mind.
    - **Be passionate about it.**

Check and rationalise –

- Are they excited by it?
- Is it within reach? It doesn't have to be easy but it needs to feel achievable to keep the motivation.
- Are they passionate about it?
- **Do they care?**

The •peoplemad success model

Think it
See it
Draw it
Write it
Want it

*Vision

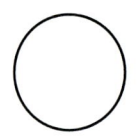

Believe it

Don't lose sight of it

*Important note:
To be the very best every single person in your team needs to want it as much as you.

'There are only two options regarding commitment. You're either in or out. There's no such thing as a life in between.'
Pat Riley, American basketball coach and motivational speaker.

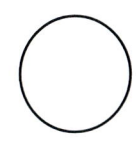

Teach your strategy and approach

The simplest definition of strategy is:

Knowing where you are today, knowing where you want to be tomorrow and having a plan to get there.

Knowing where you are today:
- See Section 7 for tips on personal performance.
- Carry out a review of where you are today – a **current state assessment.**
- Understand today's position in as much detail as possible: strengths, weaknesses, markets, products, customers, staff, systems, costs, income streams etc.
- Assess everything including people and their feelings.
- Get accurate facts and figures.
- Be truthful as to the realistic position.
- The more accurate and detailed the information the easier it will be to make decisions on what needs to change.

*To be the very best every single person in your team needs to understand what, why, how and when you are going to do things.

The •peoplemad success model

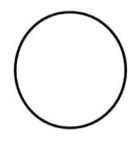

*Knowing where you want to be tomorrow

Think OUTCOME

Know where you want to be tomorrow:

- Start with your vision.
- Take your thoughts and drawings and turn them into detailed descriptions of what the future looks like.
- Think of everything especially the people.
- Remember to consider all the areas reviewed in the current state assessment.

Develop a strategy:

- Plot how to move from today's position to the described vision.
- Brainstorm ideas.
- Get other people involved especially those that are going to be impacted by the strategy.
- Get commitment and support as early as possible.
- Assess the risks and put mitigation plans in place.

*To be the very best every single person in your team needs to understand what tomorrow is going to look like and how you are going to get there.

The •peoplemad success model

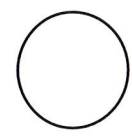

*Align personal and business objectives

- You now have a vision and a strategy – objectives will give focus to make it happen.
- Set objectives for the business, team and everyone involved.
- Make sure that the team and everyone's personal objectives are aligned to the business objectives and together deliver the strategy.
- Keep them simple.
- Make sure they are the right ones and lead you down the right path.
- Describe them in such a way that there is no doubt when they are achieved.
- Set some short term objectives – they will act as stepping stones and give a sense of achievement along the way.
- Get commitment and support – think about everyone impacted by your actions.
- Communicate progress.
- Celebrate success as each objective is achieved.

*To be the very best every single person in your team needs to show their commitment with actions and words.

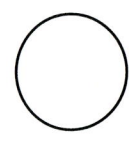

Personal plans should be aligned to the business plans

- A simple plan is a list of what you are going to do and when.
- The more people involved and the more complicated the change being undertaken then the more detailed the plan will need to be.
- Some activity will depend on other things that need to be done first – in project management land these are called dependencies.
- Think of the risks involved – they will need to be managed and they take time.
- Think of the people involved – they will need to be managed and they take time ☺.
- All plans have financial implications – think costs and budgets and align financial plans to operational plans based on activity and timelines.
- Plans need to be kept up to date and communicated.
- Planning is a skill get good at it.
- Also refer to **Pause and reflect** , *Brown paper planning, and Measure progress in Section 3.*

'Do not squander time, for that is the stuff life is made of.'
Benjamin Franklin, American statesman.

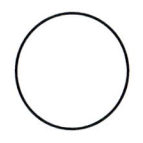

The principles of good planning

- A team's operational plans need to be aligned to the organisation's strategic plans.
- Make a list of all the things that need to be done.
- Put them in some sort of order remembering that some things might be dependent on others (e.g. if you are building a house the walls can't be built until the footings are in).
- Draw a timeline and put the actions that need to be taken under the appropriate dates.
- A trick is to start with the end date and work backwards (like planning a journey – what time do I want to get there? How long will it take? So what time do I need to leave?).
- Put in some milestones – things that can be achieved along the way to help target progress and a sense of getting to where you want to be.
- Sit back and assess whether your plan is realistic and achievable under your timescales.
- Have I missed anything? What would happen if?
- Plan, plan and plan again until you are happy.

'The best preparation for good work tomorrow is to do good work today'. **Elbert Hubbard, American businessman and writer.**

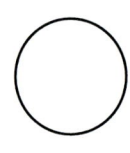

Role Definition

- Roles must be 'complementary to' not 'in competition with' each other.
- Roles must be clearly defined so that job holders fully understand:
    - What they are expected to do and the boundaries within which they are expected to operate.
    - How well they are expected to perform and the rewards that they can expect in return.
    - The contribution they are making and how their job fits into the bigger picture.
    - Each role must contribute to the overall strategy otherwise it is wasted effort.
- Sometimes boundaries have to overlap because you don't want things to fall through the gaps. Be clear to all involved who is responsible for what and when.
- Keep Role Definitions to the point and easy to understand.
- Keep Role Definitions up to date and review them in line with your regular reviews on performance to make sure nothing has changed.

'The secret to success is constancy to purpose.'
Benjamin Disraeli, British Prime Minister.

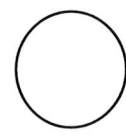

Procedures

- The Oxford English Dictionary definition is: ***A series of actions conducted in a certain order or manner; established or official way of doing something.***

- Procedures need to be well written:
    - Concise
    - Logical steps
    - Easy to read
    - Easy to understand
- Procedures should:
    - Reflect best practice
    - Be followed without exception
    - Be part of training – especially Induction
- Keep them relevant.
- Continually review procedures to see if there is a better way of doing things.
- Keep them simple
    - The more complicated something is then the more chance there is of it going wrong and the more costly it will be to put right.

The •peoplemad success model

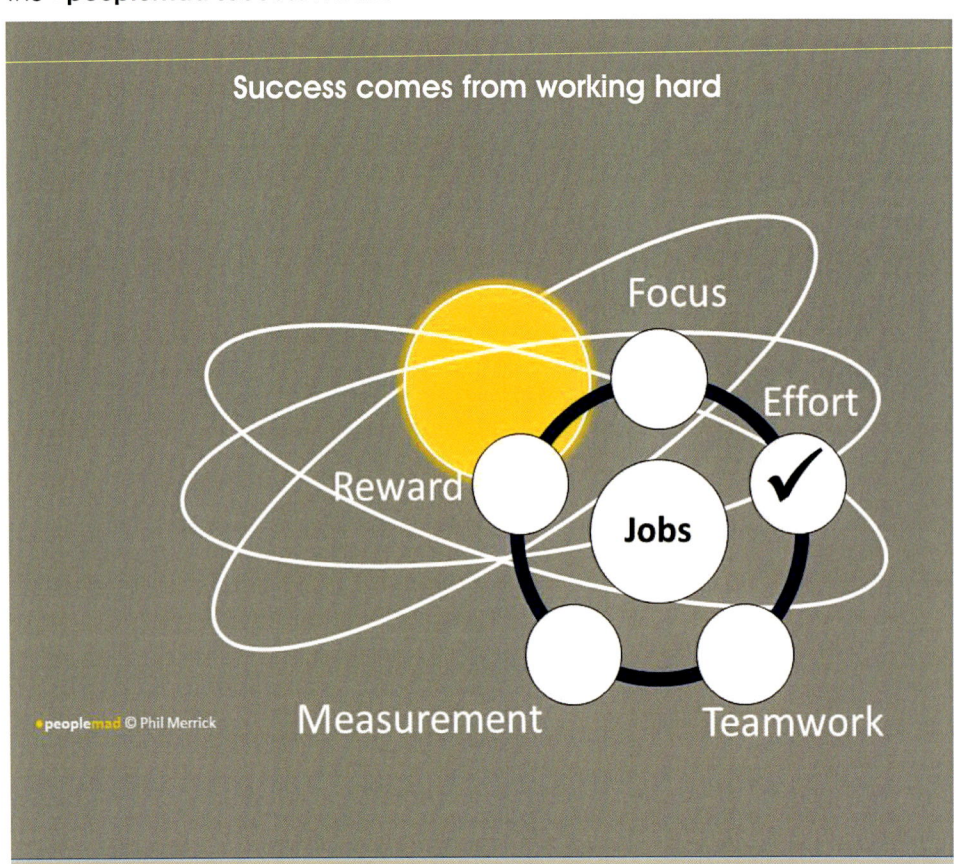

Success comes from working hard

- Focus
- Effort
- Jobs
- Reward
- Measurement
- Teamwork

•peoplemad © Phil Merrick

100% effort

100% quality

100% time

WORK IN PROGRESS

The •peoplemad success model

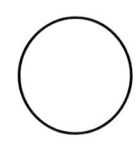

Michelangelo, Italian painter and sculptor, said:

'If people knew how hard I work to gain my mastery, it would not seem so wonderful at all.'

Nothing was ever achieved without hard work.
Talent alone is not enough – If you follow football you'll know that the great Barcelona team as skilled as they are, work harder than anyone, always closing down the opposition when they don't have the ball. They work and they work and they work.

No one person is more important than the other – they just have different jobs and that includes the manager, supervisor, team captain… whoever.

I heard a great story about a group of school children visiting NASA at the Kennedy Space Centre, Florida.
There was a guy there sweeping the floor. The teacher asked him what he did at the Space Centre and he replied:

'I help put people on the moon.'

How great is that? He believes that all his effort and hard work contribute to the vision – and of course he's right.

The •peoplemad success model

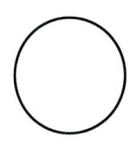

Contribution

Think OUTCOME

- The Oxford English Dictionary definition is: ***that which is given in order to help achieve or provide something.***

- The key word in the definition is 'help' – contribution is about giving something towards the bigger picture along with other people.
- The sum of the parts equals the whole – be clear who needs to contribute what.
- Be specific about your expectations
    - What needs to be done?
    - How will it be done?
    - How well will it be done?
    - Where will it be done?
    - By when will it be finished?
- Get people working together in harmony to achieve the common goal.
- Encourage focus, minimise distraction and interruption.

The ideal contribution is:

100% effort

100% quality for

100% of the time.

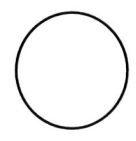

Contribution: Performance Management

- Performance Management in some organisations is just about setting targets and paying out bonuses.
- Performance Management should be about recognising people's strengths and weaknesses and helping them perform to their very best.
- Setting targets gives people something to strive for.
- Paying out bonuses (not necessarily cash) can be an extra inducement to achieve success.
- Be very careful to reward people fairly across the teams.
- Performance Management is People Management – nurture and grow your team and you will nurture and grow your business.
- Make expectations and the method of measurement clear at the outset so that there is no room for subjectivity in the assessment of performance.
- Use the SMART technique for setting targets.
- Use KPI's for measuring performance.
- Use the SENSIBLE technique for paying out bonuses.

- See Measurement later in this section.

The •peoplemad success model

Tools
also see Thinking Tools in section 9

Think OUTCOME

- The Oxford English Dictionary definition is: ***A thing used to help perform a job.***
- Get the right tools
    - –The right design to do the best job.
    - –The right design for safety.
    - –Keep them up to date.
    - –Don't skimp on quality.
    - –Keep them at optimum performance.
- Don't think of tools as just equipment and machinery. Tools are anything that you use to help you do a job e.g. tennis racket, mobile phone, goal-keeping gloves, computer software.
- Better tools = better performance, especially where there is a greater reliance on tools to do the job e.g. cycling.
- Buying the most expensive tools does not mean they are the best – it just means they are the most expensive.
- Science and technology is advancing all the time – keep abreast of developments.
- Giving people the right tools helps to make people feel valued. As we say throughout this handbook 'people perform better when they feel good about themselves'.

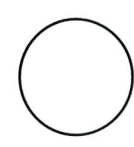

Training

- The Oxford English Dictionary definition is: **Teach a skill or type of behaviour through regular practise and instruction.**

- Training motivates and makes people feel valued.
- It helps with team bonding, especially when it's linked to a common goal.
- Have a plan for you, your team, your organisation.
- Make it specific to your needs – carry out a training needs analysis.
- Make it focused, measure results.
- Assess performance and give constructive feedback.
- Monitor progress against the plan and plan again.
- Take your training to a live environment only when you're happy with it.
- Give new people induction training. This is invaluable for improving performance and sends a strong message that training is important.
- Always train with a purpose.
- Link training to practise – learn something, practise it.
- Train, practise, train, practise, train, practise…

The •peoplemad success model

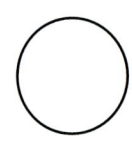

Training: practise

Think OUTCOME

- The Oxford English Dictionary definition is: **Perform an activity or exercise a skill repeatedly or regularly in order to acquire, maintain, or improve proficiency in it.**
- When you learn a skill you use your conscious brain to understand and apply that skill until through practise it becomes automatic and part of your subconscious (like driving a car).
- Your brain is essentially conditioned to perform that skill in a certain way through practise.
- Practise the right technique and you are conditioning yourself to succeed – practise the wrong technique and you are conditioning yourself to fail.
- Successful people practise more than unsuccessful people.
- Practise is not an optional exercise – make it disciplined, focused, targeted and work hard at it.
- Practise, practise, practise.

'That's why he practises so much'.
Jonathan Davies 17th March 2012. Commentating on Leigh Halfpenny's 52 metre penalty kick which gave Wales 13-6 lead against France at the Millennium Stadium in Cardiff. Halfpenny kicked another penalty late in the game and Wales went on to win 16-9 winning the Grand Slam.

The •peoplemad success model

Teamwork

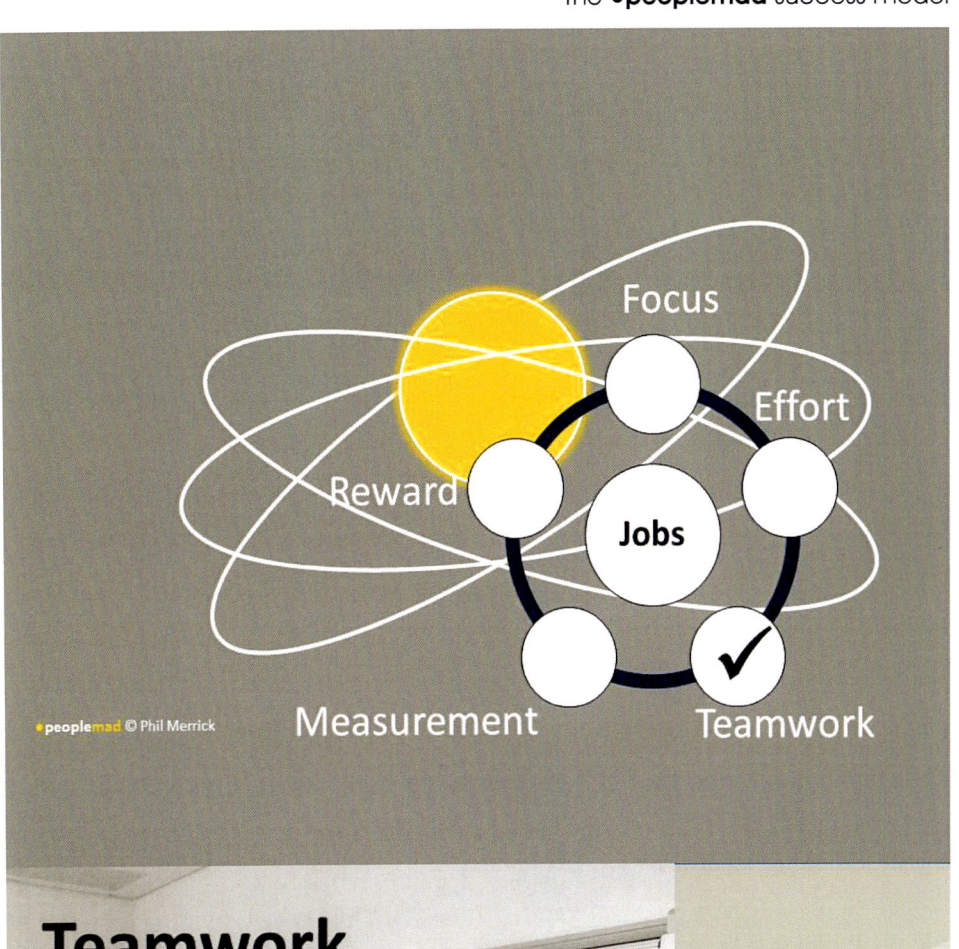

'To come together to achieve a common goal'

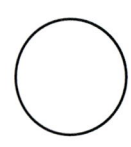

Teamwork

- The Oxford English Dictionary definition is:
    - **–two or more people working together**
    - **– a group of players forming one side in a competitive game or sport**
    - –Verb: to come together to **achieve a common goal**
- Teamwork needs a special mention because the power of people pulling together epitomises the second rule of •**peoplemad** – surround yourself with the right people.
- Teams work well when they have:
    - –A common objective
    - –Complimentary skills
    - –Camaraderie
    - **–The right people doing the right things**
    - –A strong leader
- People in a team have to be able to get on – they do not need to like each other, but it helps.
- No one person is more important than the other – they just have different jobs.
- Don't put up with anyone who is not a team player or has a disruptive influence – you are better off without them.

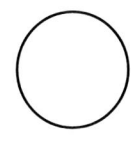

Define your team(s)

- An organisation will have a number of teams each with their own specific role all working together to achieve the organisation's objectives.

- You should know how your team fits into the overall operating model of the organisation.

- It is very likely that the structure of the organisation will mean that you are in more than one team.

- For example in the following diagram the people in Team 11 are also in the larger Teams 9, 4 and 1.

- It is important that they know what is going on in the larger structure.

- It is important that they are made to feel part of what is going on in the larger structure.

- You will need to think about how you align objectives, how you reward people and importantly how you communicate to make sure that all the teams work together and everyone is fully committed.

The •peoplemad success model

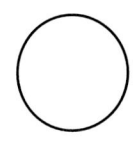

Define your team(s)

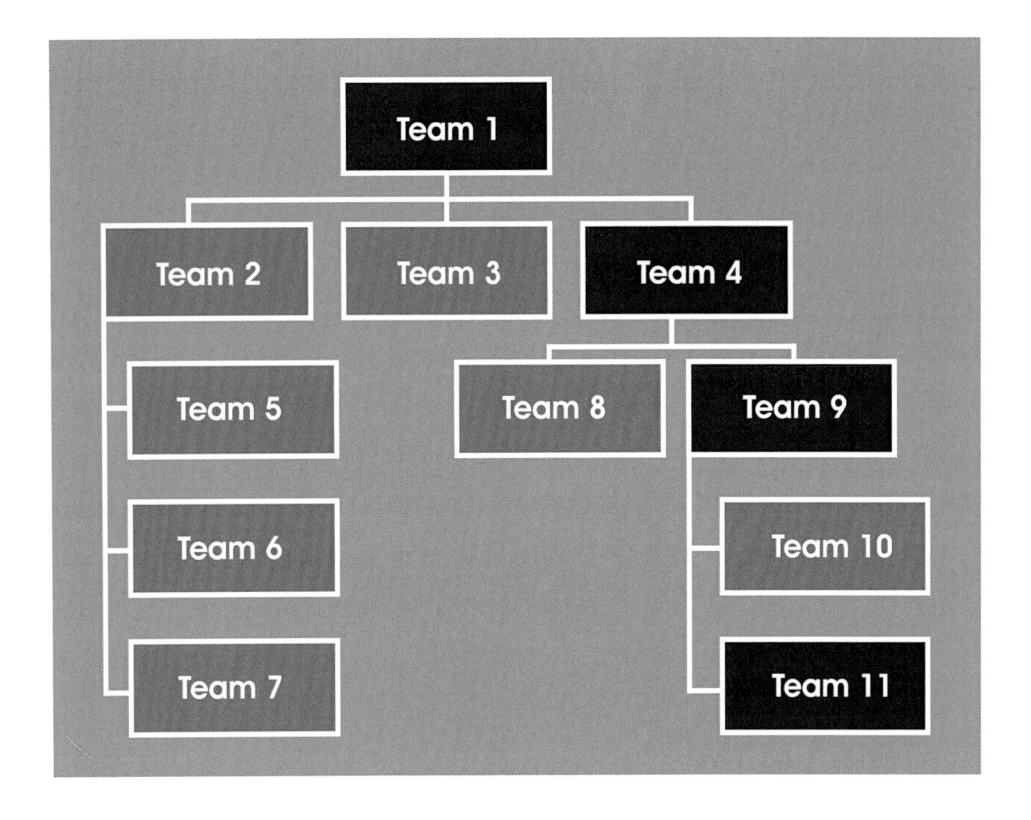

		Team 1		
Team 2		Team 3		Team 4
— Team 5			Team 8	Team 9
— Team 6				— Team 10
— Team 7				— Team 11

In a typical operating structure people can be part of a number of different teams. In this example people in team 11 are also in the larger teams 9, 4 and 1.

The •**peoplemad** success model

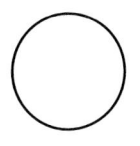

○ **Disparate teams need to be aligned**

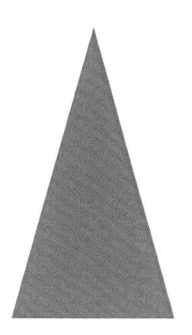

Different Strategies? Goals? Plans? Policies? Guiding Principles?

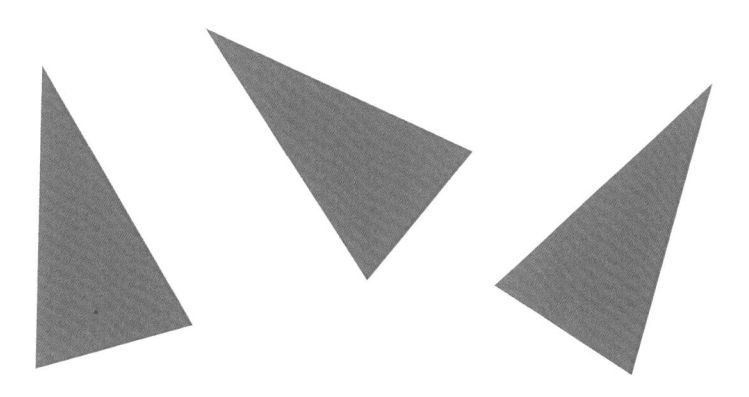

The •peoplemad success model

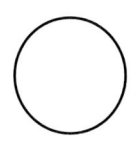

All heading in the same direction

Structure
Order
Control
Consistency
Purpose
Belonging

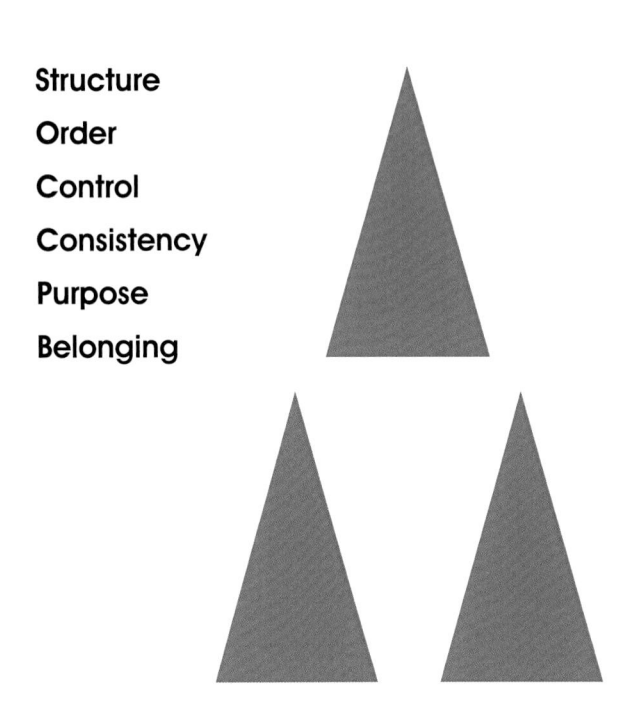

Common Strategies, Goals, Plans, Policies, Guiding Principles.

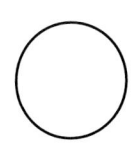

'You can only get a result out there if you've got total togetherness and total belief in each other.' Graeme Souness, European Cup winner with Liverpool in 1978, 1981, 1984.

Talking about Chelsea's 2-2 draw at the Nou Camp in the Champions League semi final against Barcelona, the best team in the World, to go through to the final. Chelsea had skipper John Terry sent off with 50 minutes to go and came back from 2 nil down. April 2012.

'The best way to find out if you can trust somebody is to trust them.'
Ernest Hemingway, American author.

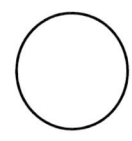

Teamwork: delegation

- The Oxford English Dictionary definition is: ***A person sent or authorised to represent others; entrust a task or responsibility to others***
- Delegation is an effective way to share workloads.
- Make sure the person being delegated to has the right capability to perform the task to the expected standard.
- Be clear about exactly what is being delegated.
- Agree scope, quality, outcome and timescales.
- You can delegate responsibility for something but you must remain accountable.
- Stay interested in the task and monitor progress.
- Give feedback on how well it was done.
- Delegation when done properly can be an effective part of someone's development programme.
- Offer help and advice where needed but allow people the chance to show what they can do for themselves.
- Delegation of work to others is not one of the perks of being a boss. It is a tool to manage work effectively and it must be done properly and for the right reasons.

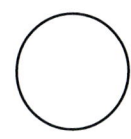

Trying to fit everyone in

- This is a common mistake in sports management.

- In a team situation the best scenario is that you have the best people, experts in their specialist positions, all performing to their very best.

- Because a manager needs cover in case of injury or suspension he/she will often have a large squad of players all competing for a position in the team.

- There has been many an occasion where a manager has all the best players available and tries to find a position for them all – not necessarily playing everyone in the positions that suit them best.

- These decisions mean that the best people are not being used to their full capability and the team is not playing to its full potential as a result.

- It can also cause upset for the other players who have been left out and feel they warrant their place.

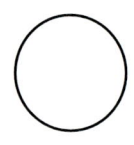

A football analogy: using good players to 'fill-in'

- If someone is injured then putting in a direct replacement will mean that one position might be a bit weaker but it has not disrupted the overall structure of the team.

- Some managers, however, move a player who is very good in one position to cover in another position because he/she is good enough to 'fill-in', effectively weakening two positions.

- England Captain Steven Gerrard was often used on the right hand side of midfield for Liverpool and left hand side for England even though he was one of the best central midfield players in the World.

Another example is at the left back (and left wing) position where there is often a scarcity of good players. Some managers move the recognised right back across to fill-in if the left back gets injured, effectively weakening two positions disrupting 50% of the defence (if you're playing four at the back).

'Let every man practise the profession that he knows best.'
Marcu Tullius Cicero, Roman statesman and orator.

The •peoplemad success model

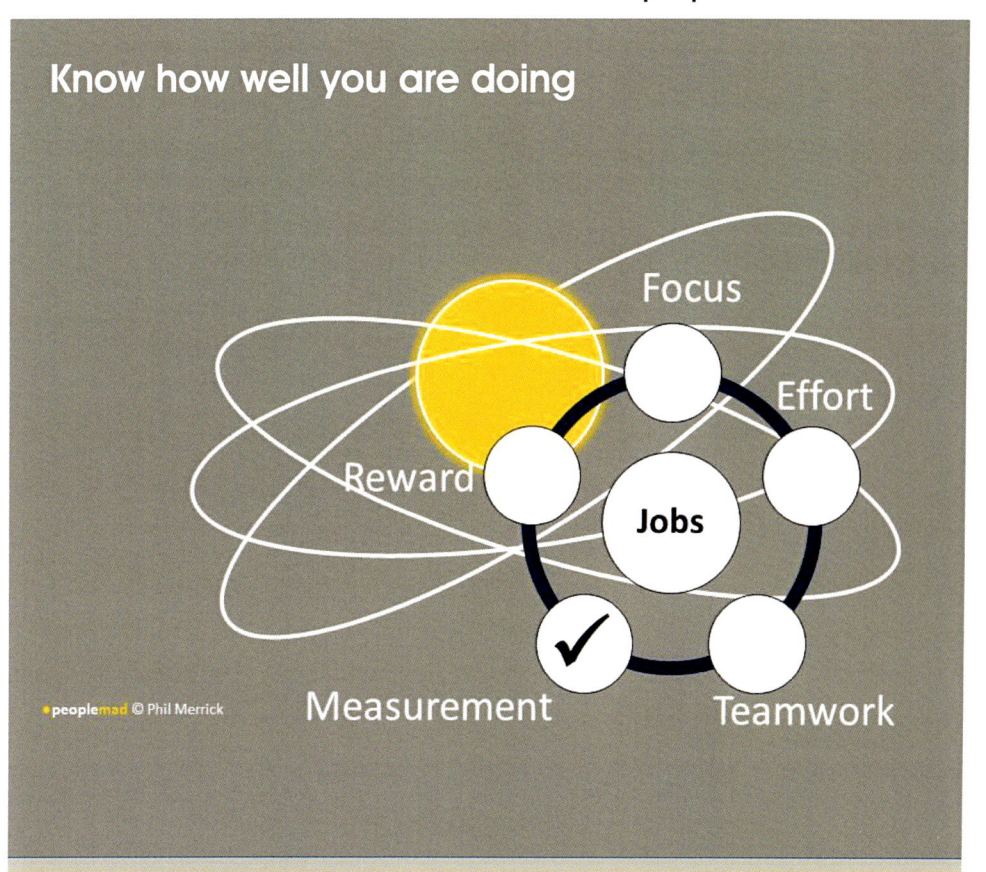

Know how well you are doing

peoplemad © Phil Merrick

Focus
Effort
Reward
Jobs
Measurement
Teamwork

Measure what's important

Targets
Objectives
KPI's
Financials

Emotional well being!

The ●peoplemad success model

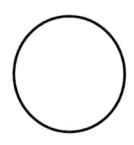

Measurement: Key Performance Indicators

- Think high level monitoring of what is going on in my business.

- Improvement to all round performance will require measurement and feedback on a number of different areas.

- KPI's are a set of quantifiable measures that gauge and compare the performance of an organisation in terms of meeting strategic and operational goals.

- Think of KPI's as indicators for different aspects of performance like a dashboard on a motor car.

- The word 'Key' is important – just focus on a few areas.

- Limit them to those factors that are essential to the organisation reaching its goals e.g. sales, customer relationships, customer service.

- Keep everyone's attention focused on achieving the same KPIs.

- These should be continually reviewed in line with performance to encourage new behaviours and activity.

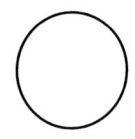

Measurement: achievement of objectives

- The definition of Performance as per the Encarta English Dictionary is: **The way in which somebody does a job, judged by its effectiveness.**

- In order to measure the effectiveness of a performance there has to have been a level of expectation laid down at the start – your set of targets and objectives.

- Define what success looks like.

- Naturally the more specific the objectives the easier it is to assess whether or not they have been achieved.

- How did you expect to perform? How well did you do?

- You, your team and your organisation should all have a plan of action to improve performance over time. These performance plans drive performance based on the vision, strategy and objectives.

'If everyone is moving forward together then success takes care of itself.' **Henry Ford, American motor manufacturer.**

The •peoplemad success model

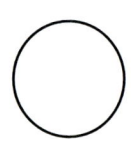

Objectives: setting targets

Think OUTCOME

- There are numerous models for setting and managing targets. SMART is one of the most well known, is as good as anything else and is simple to use.

SMART - make sure your targets are:
- Specific
- Measurable
- Achievable
- Realistic
- Timely

- For paying out bonuses you should use this model:

- **SENSIBLE:**
    - Keep them small relative to basic pay.
    - Make sure they drive the right behaviours.
- Always think about the outcome you want to achieve – will your targets make it happen?

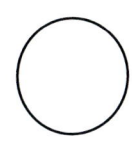

High level financial planning

- In simple terms this is about managing your finances in line with whatever activity you plan to carry out.
- The main areas to consider are:
    - The overall impact on the profit and loss account.
    - The need to manage the cash flow – the timing of money coming in and money going out.
- Your budget: the whole point of budgeting is to give an idea of what you expect to receive (income) and spend (costs).
- A simple spreadsheet will often suffice for a high level financial plan.
- If you are planning for a project then align the budget to the timeline of the project – and beyond if you want to keep a record of related income and costs that continue after the project has gone live.
- Income due to be generated as a result of the project should be planned and recorded separately to the running of the project.
- Use 'what if' scenarios to plan. What if this happens? What if I do this?
- Think about the **OUTCOME** that you want for **all** your decisions.

The •peoplemad success model

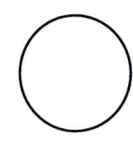

High level financial monitoring

Think OUTCOME

There are a lot of business owners who do not know how well they are doing until they speak to their accountants. This is high risk and can end in tears. It is important to find a way of knowing your figures ideally on a daily basis (even if they are only ball park) and have a system for projecting forward so you know how well your business will fair in the future. This is where good management accountants come in – they are worth their weight in gold (assuming of course they are appropriate for your size of business). They will prepare this information for you which can help with critical informed decisions on how to run your business.

Keep your own 'back of a fag packet' notes on what you are going to get in and what you are going to spend – it will help you keep on top of things.

- Keep your finger on the pulse.

- know how your business is doing.

- Know the financial consequences of every decision before you make them.

The •peoplemad success model

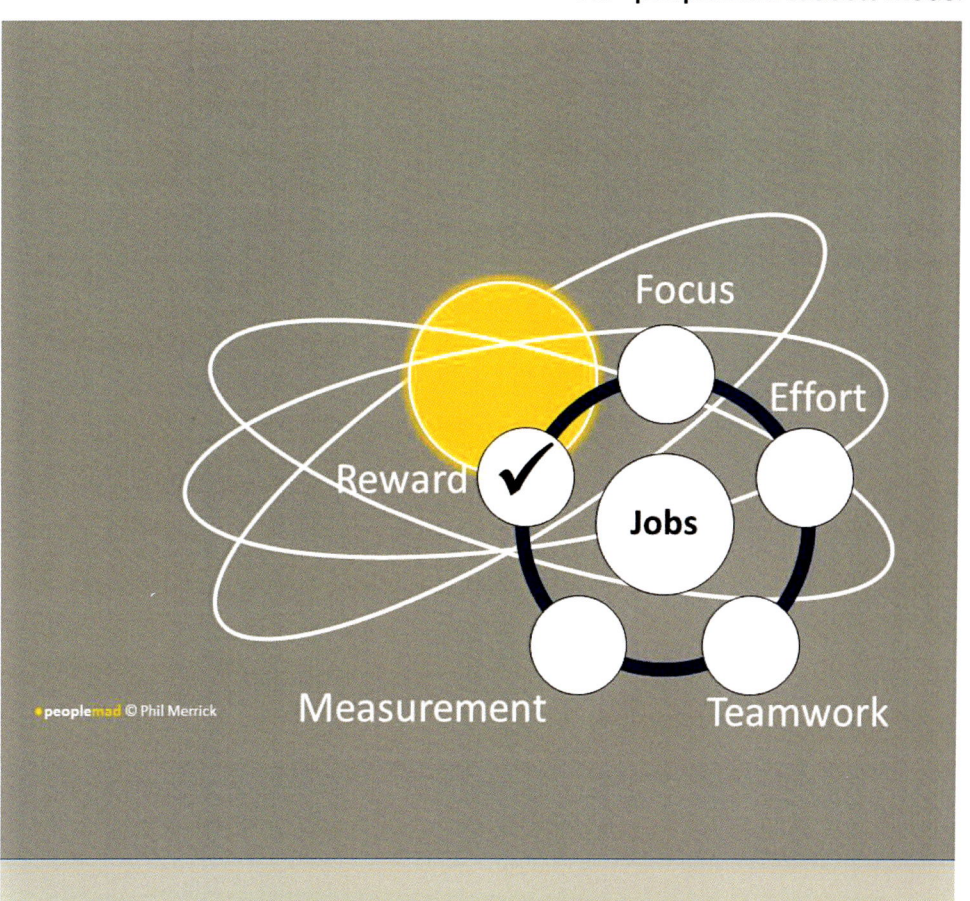

Reward performance

The •peoplemad success model

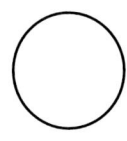

Recognition

- The Oxford English Dictionary definition is: ***A thing given in recognition of service, effort or achievement.***
- Reward can take many forms – usually cash, but never forget gifts, time off and importantly praise.
- Recognition for an achievement is very motivational.
- Think carefully about how people are given recognition
    - –if it is done properly it can motivate the rest of the team – I want that.
    - –If it is done badly it can demotivate the rest of the team – what about me?
- Remember people perform better when they feel good about themselves and being fairly rewarded is key (see Leadership).
- To be 'fairly rewarded' consideration needs to be given to the job in hand, how well it is being performed and how much other people are being paid as well.
- Get the balance right between incentives and basic pay.
- If you are paying a salary for someone to do a good job then a bonus should be exceptional – when someone has gone the extra mile.
- If a bonus is linked to a targeted performance then this should still be small relative to salary (see Risks).

- **Make sure incentives drive the right behaviours.**

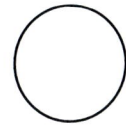

Risks

- Where people's livelihood depends on being successful they are likely to take risks when things aren't going well to make sure that they stay in a job.

- Bonuses should only form a small percentage of the total package to avoid desperate measures if targets aren't likely to be achieved.

- Be very careful what you incentivise. For example there is a huge difference between increasing market share and trying to get profitable market share.

- Don't rely on the people at the top to be the risk controllers – these guys stand or fall by their results and have a vested interest in getting good figures.

- Reward the right behaviours

    – desperate sales people willing to rip off customers to get their bonuses?
    – **Or** professional executives providing a tip-top service enhancing your reputation.

- Know your subject, learn from the past. Think risk.

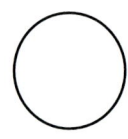

Leadership tips

- Even if you have the right people it is wasted effort if you have them doing the wrong things.
- Think about the strategy – is everything focused on achieving your aims?
- How much effort is wasted?
- Give people the right training – avoid continual sheep dipping (giving the same training to everyone).
- Give people the right tools.
- You can delegate work but you can't delegate accountability.
- Always check the objectives to see if a job is being done properly or worth being done at all: 'what is it we are trying to achieve?'
- Align the development of your people to the development of your organisation.
- Don't cut training budgets when times are hard. Never sacrifice the future.
- Keep things simple.

'Any intelligent fool can make things bigger and more complex. It takes a touch of genius and a lot of courage to move in the opposite direction.'
Albert Einstein.

The •**peoplemad** success model

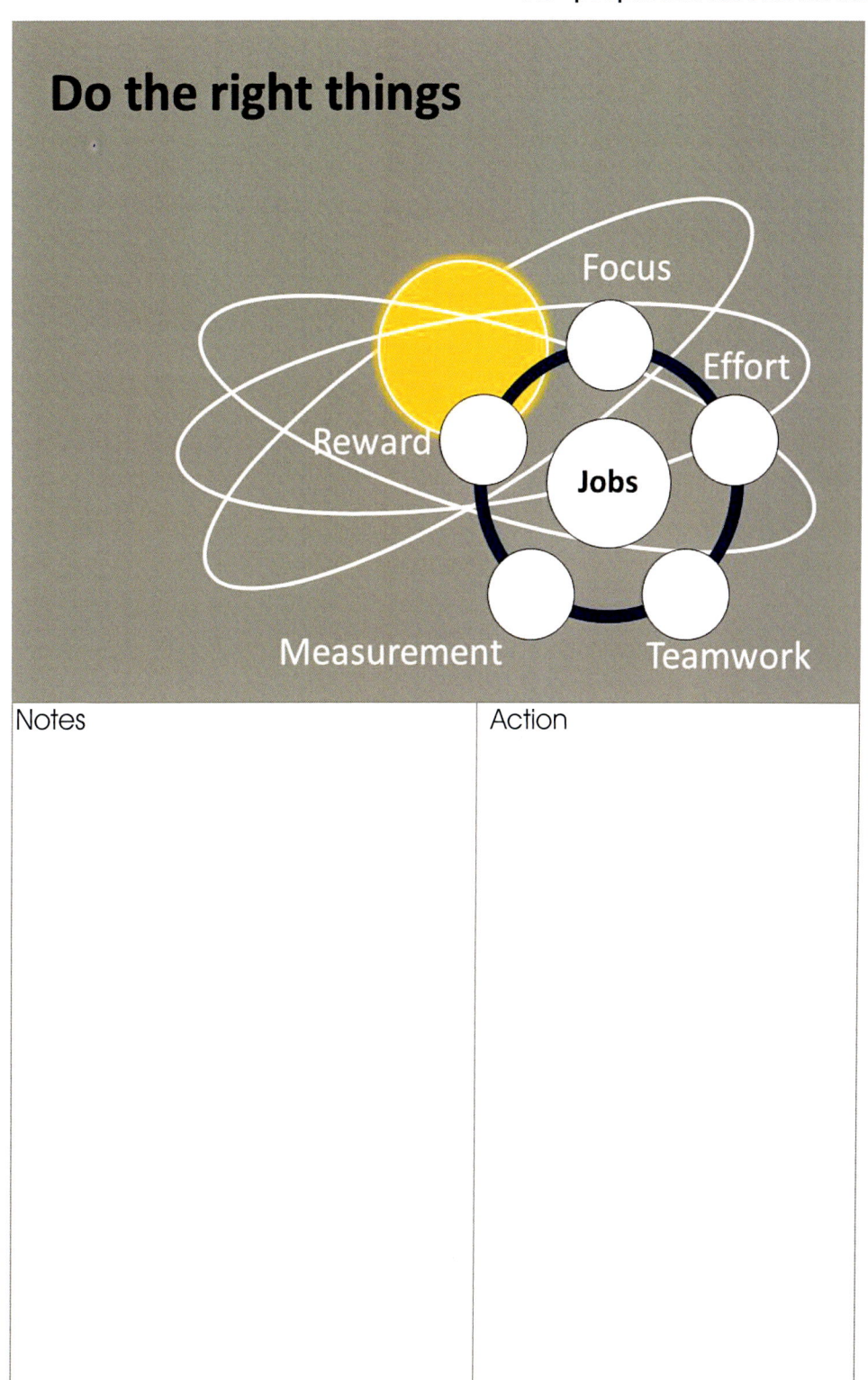

Do the right things

Focus
Effort
Reward
Jobs
Measurement
Teamwork

Notes

Action

Your own •**peoplemad** notes

The •**peoplemad** success model

6. Create the right environment

In this section:

- The •**peoplemad** success model
- Getting the environment right
- People perform better when they feel good about themselves
- Culture is the glue…
- Enjoyment
- Co-operation
- Guiding Principles
- Guiding Principles – some important points
- Controls are a benefit not a burden
- Governance
- Risk Management
- Managing risk is a continual process
- Impact on other people
- Standards
- Process
- Rules
- Rules: discipline
- Policy

Create the right environment continued

In this section continued:
- Effective communication is critical
- Communication
- Communication: meetings
- Communication: feedback
- Make your place the best place
- The best place to be
- Structure gives order and clarity
- Structure
- Leadership tips
- Your own •**peoplemad** notes

'The post match party was important, and the venue was crucial, because many of the senior staff at Barcelona feel that the real golden moment is when the full FC Barcelona family is together – staff, players, directors plus assorted parents, girlfriends, wives, children and special guests – celebrating a year's hard work.'
Graham Hunter, from his book 'Barca - the making of the best team in the World'.

The •peoplemad success model

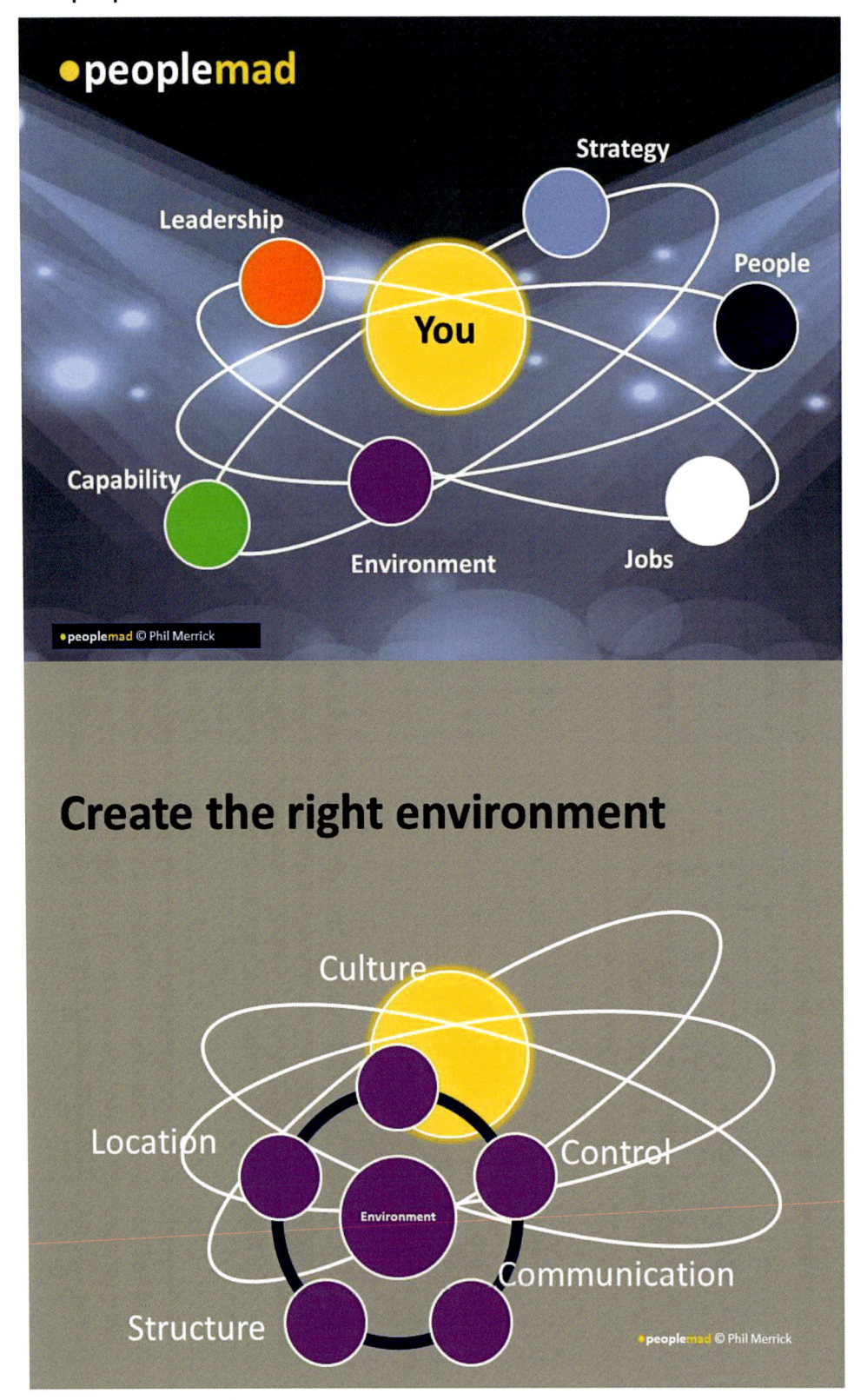

•peoplemad

- Leadership
- Strategy
- You
- People
- Capability
- Environment
- Jobs

•peoplemad © Phil Merrick

Create the right environment

- Culture
- Location
- Control
- Environment
- Communication
- Structure

•peoplemad © Phil Merrick

Getting the environment right

People perform better when they feel good about themselves so creating the right conditions will help them to work at their best.

This is the general environment and much more than just the physical location where the activity is taking place.

This is as much about culture, atmosphere and rules as it is about having a coffee machine and a potted plant on your desk.

If you've ever seen a successful team with 'something special' then this is a big part of what made them superior and gave them the edge.

If you've got highly capable people doing the right things then when you create the right conditions that allow them to flourish you've got yourself something very special.

Put the right infrastructure in place, give people the right guidance and support and then allow them to grow and perform at their very best.

Think about every single part of your business and everyone involved, including customers.

Support them with an open hand.

Where are we working? Does it help us get the best results? The office, shop floor, gymnasium, sales room, running track, class room, training pitch… is the lighting right, the equipment, the temperature? All conducive to delivering the very best results?

Whether its about maximising sales or training to be the next World champion the principles are exactly the same.

The •peoplemad success model

People perform better when they feel good about themselves

People feel good about themselves when they:

- Are treated with respect.
- Enjoy what they are doing.
- Know the rules and boundaries within which they operate.
- Know the level of performance that's expected of them.
- Believe in what they are being asked to do.
- Have the right skills, experience and knowledge for the job in hand.
- Are fairly rewarded for their activity and behaviour.
- Can see their contribution to the big picture.
- Feel that they are making a difference.
- Have a sense of belonging.
- Have certainty about their future.
- Like the people with whom they have to live, work and deal.
- Are surrounded by other people who feel good about themselves.
- **Are successful at what they do.**

This theme is embedded in the **•peoplemad** success model and is mentioned here because the environment is critical. Great leadership is what really makes it happen which of course is key to getting the culture right.

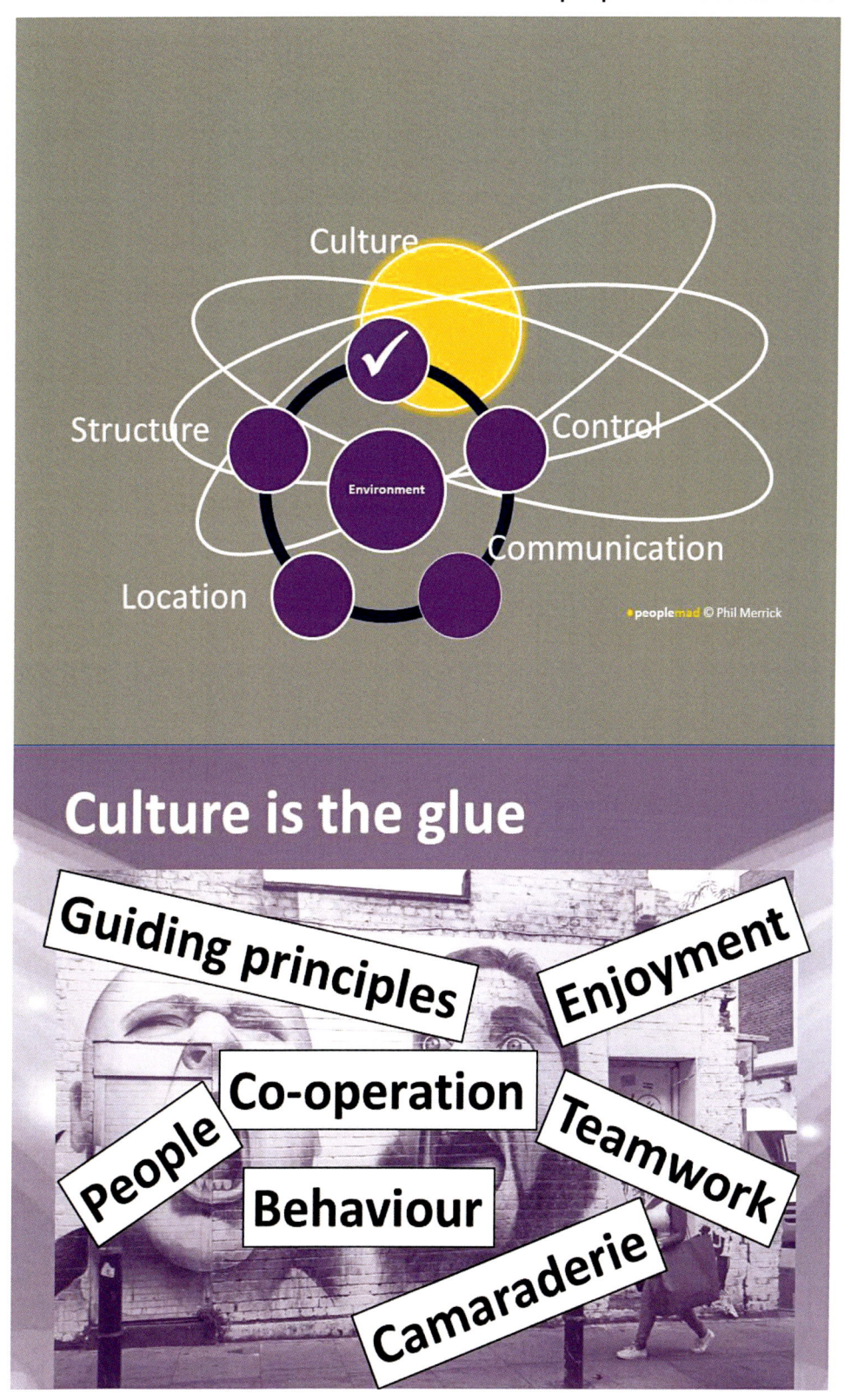

The •peoplemad success model

Culture is the glue

Guiding principles
Enjoyment
Co-operation
Teamwork
People
Behaviour
Camaraderie

The ●peoplemad success model

I love this subject. Culture is the glue that binds everything together. If you've ever seen a successful team with that 'something special' then this is that 'je ne sais quoi' that gives them the edge.

If you've got highly capable people doing the right things then when you create the right conditions that allow them to flourish you've got yourself something very special.

And a piece of advice if you're ever involved in mergers or takeovers – never force an old culture on to new people.

Create a new culture that everyone feels part of, that they themselves have helped create. It takes time of course but that's part of getting it right.

Whilst it's mainly the people that make the culture the physical environment plays a huge part as well.

It's no coincidence that the City of Sheffield Athletic Club have the best coaches and state of the art facilities and that Olympic Gold medallist Jessica Ennis-Hill just happens to comes from Sheffield*. A great athlete who had the capability to be Olympic Champion wherever she was born but the local environment helped her to develop her talents. How many other Olympic Champions might we have across the country that we'll never know about because they don't have the right environment in which to flourish?

*Incidentally Yorkshire and England cricketer Joe Root went to the same school in Sheffield as Jessica Ennis-Hill. The school must have some great sports teachers.

Enjoyment

- The Oxford English Dictionary definition is: ***The state or process of taking pleasure in something.***
- See 'sense of humour' in Section 4.
- Laughter is an enjoyable experience – it raises spirits and makes people feel good about themselves.
- Being able to laugh at things releases tension.
- Humour is a big part of team camaraderie.

CAUTION:
- –team camaraderie often involves 'mickey taking', there is a limit to what is acceptable and it must not be cruel and divisive.
- –Work must be taken seriously and humour must not detract from the job at hand.
- –Always respect your colleagues, their workloads and their personal circumstances.

- You need to be able to laugh at yourself- it helps with team spirit.
- Work hard, play hard, have fun.
- Celebrate success.

'The most wasted day is that in which we have not laughed.'
Sebastian Roch Nicolas Chamfort, French writer.

Co-operation

The Oxford English Dictionary definition is: Work together towards the same end; help someone or comply with their requests.

- The act of co-operating is fundamental to building relationships and working with other people.
- Co-operation is not:
    - 'Giving in' to someone.
    - Doing something because you've been told to.
    - A sign of weakness.

Co-operation is:
   - Doing something that helps both / all parties.
   - A quick way of getting something done.
   - A sign of strength.
- Collaborate – helping someone else with their performance can help you with yours – a *win, win* situation.

'A small group of thoughtful people could change the World. Indeed, it's the only thing that ever has.'
Margaret Mead, American cultural anthropologist.

Guiding Principles

- Have some guiding principles on expected behaviours (a *Code of Conduct* is similar but implies a set of rules rather than a set of values) see Rules: discipline.
- The Oxford English Dictionary definition:
    - **–Values:** *principles or standards of behaviour.*
    - **–Morals:** *principles of right or wrong.*
- **Values and morals** are beliefs about behaviour and what you perceive to be the difference between right and wrong.
- If different people in your team have different values / morals this is likely to cause conflict.
- Naturally people feely strongly about their values / morals and might not be prepared to change – which means the related behaviour will continue.
- The best teams have shared values:
    - –agree them together.
    - –keep them simple.
    - –get buy in and ownership from everyone.
- Stick to your principles - stay strong when they are tested.

'Integrity is the essence of everything successful.'
Richard Fuller, American author.

Guiding Principles – some important points

- Guiding principles are not a 'nice to have', they play a very important role in improving the performance of your team and organisation.
- Be very careful about your wording and interpretation of the meaning. If you say 'the Customer is always right' then your policies and processes need to reflect just that.
    - –for example: customers services, complaints, returns policy
- Make them sincere. 'We trust and respect each other' are fine words but they have to be meant and again need to be reflected in your policies and processes.
    - –for example: HR manuals, Code of conduct, Disciplinary policy
- Design your Guiding Principles to drive the right behaviours.
- Importantly your principles need to be live and demonstrated across the organisation through behaviour.
- It starts at the top – your leaders lead through their actions and words and these MUST reflect your guiding principles.
- Make them visible – put them on posters, talk about them, be proud of them. Let everyone know including your customers.

The •peoplemad success model

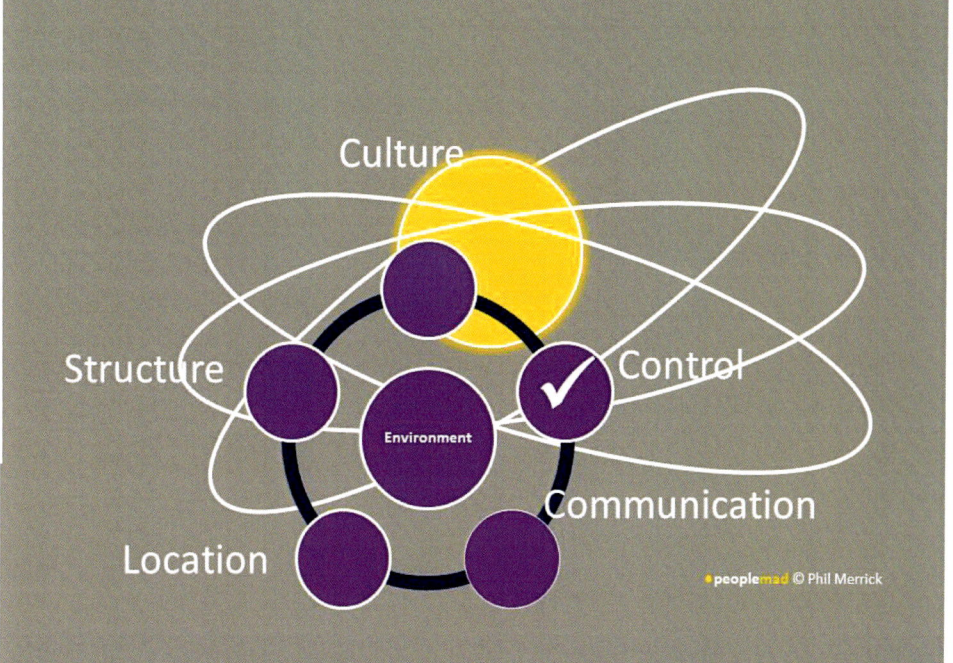

Controls are a benefit not a burden

Governance
Standards
Codes
Rules
Policies
Risk

The •peoplemad success model

You must have a controls. You need governance, risk management, standards, rules and policies telling people this is the way we do things around here. They need to be clear and simple; they don't have to be heavy handed but people need to work in a controlled environment. Naturally if you work in the Nuclear Power industry your needs are going to be different to (say) working in a florists, but the principles are the same. It starts at the very top. Your legal structure and operating structures need to be right for your type of business (see Structure). You need to be absolutely clear who is responsible for running the business and who makes sure it doesn't take unnecessary risk – very often they are the same person, which in itself is a risk. As employers and employees we want to be happy that we are protected from risk. Controls give a feeling of security and certainty as well as being a critical function of the day to day operation of the business.

The Head of Audit at British Airways used to remind people about the law of entropy – everything falls into dis-array unless checked. That's because controls are taken for granted. We forget to check that they're working; we don't have time, we get complacent because nothing has gone wrong. It's only when there's a scare that people worry about them. Like the Heartbleed virus made thousands of people change their passwords. Did you know that the Cyber crime market generates more revenue for the criminals than the drug trafficking market? World wide.

The •peoplemad success model

One of the biggest worries for most businesses is fraud. In a well run operation there are usually back up controls so for things to go badly wrong more than one control has to be breached. That's why collusion between two or more people is difficult to stop. When I ran the Audit team we had a tip off by the Police that a fraud ring was targeting our Bank. We were told we had been infiltrated by a security guard, an IT specialist and a senior accounts clerk – giving access to buildings, computer systems, customer accounts and bank accounts. Now, as far as collusion is concerned this is a very potent cocktail of people. We put a small team together, worked around the clock and set up specific reports to check for any abnormal activity… and we waited, and waited.. and waited. Nothing happened. Very pleased with ourselves we reported back to the CEO and the main Board on all the possible ways that the fraud team could get money out of the system and all the extra controls that we'd put in place to prevent it from happening. We then realised that this report was dynamite if it got into the wrong hands. It was effectively a manual telling any would-be fraudster how to rob the bank. So after all our hard work, the report, all the files and reams and reams of working papers were destroyed. At least that's what we told the Board ☺.

Governance

- The Oxford English Dictionary definition is: *The action or manner of governing; conducting the policy or affairs; control or influence.*
- Keep governance (the management of policies, standards, control) completely separate from operational activity.
- Give governance and operational roles to different people e.g. keep the Chairman and Chief Executive Officer as separate roles
    - The CEO runs the operation on a day to day basis.
    - The Chairman has responsibility to shareholders / members to make sure the CEO and his Executive Team don't take undue risks.
- Non - Executive Directors have a responsibility to ensure the organisation doesn't take undue risk.
- If you have an Internal Audit function make sure it is completely independent from the day to day operation.
- Use an Audit Committee (with external Audit and non – exec Director representation) to monitor the effectiveness of the Internal Audit function.
- It is your responsibility to know what is going on in your organisation. Stay close to your Accountants and Auditors whether in house or out sourced.

Risk Management

- Create a risk management culture:
    - −Speak openly about risks and actions taken.
    - −Create a process to manage them.
    - −Keep it simple.
- The risks associated with taking any action should always be assessed.
- For most things in life we do it automatically.
- For projects and large scale change then risk assessment should be a conscious effort and form part of your project management discipline.
- The level of mitigating action will be determined by how much risk you are prepared to take.
- Risks need to be assessed and managed on a continual basis not as a one off event.
- What could go wrong?
- What do we need to do to stop it going wrong?
- What would be the impact if it did go wrong?
- Think of the impact especially on people, time and cost.
- Take responsibility for managing the risks of your business – stay close to your staff and the finances. No shocks.

Managing risk is a continual process

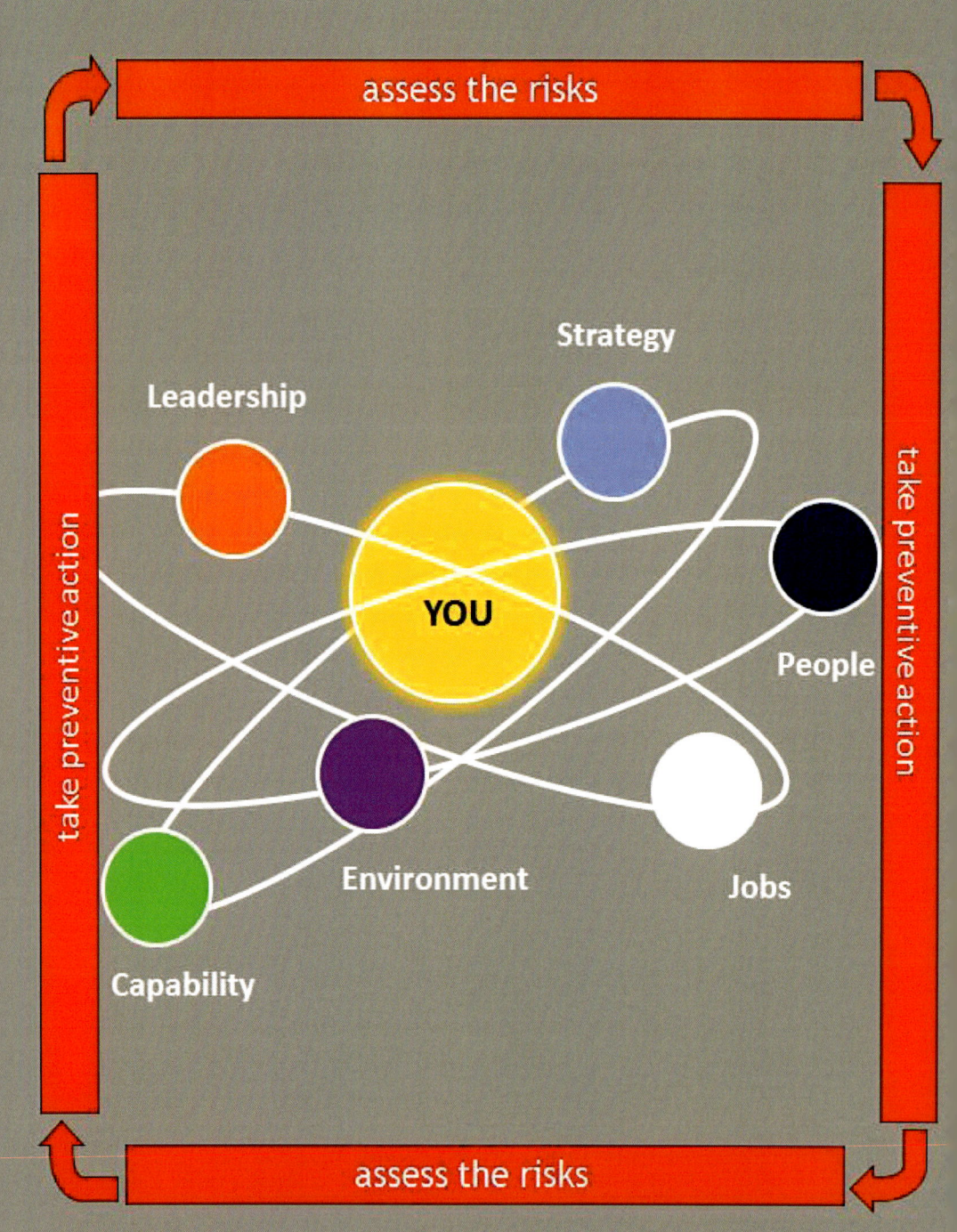

assess the risks

take preventive action

Leadership

Strategy

YOU

People

Capability

Environment

Jobs

take preventive action

assess the risks

Impact on other people

- Whenever you are making decisions and taking action it will invariably affect other people.

- People will be affected directly and indirectly, so make sure you fully understand the reach of your action(s), including the 'knock-on effect'.

- Think about the effect you are having on everyone's lives and think about the emotional impact.

- Remember that you need other people to make things work.

- Think carefully about what you say and how you say it.

- This holds true for everyday life situations but is magnified in times of change.

'If the young are not initiated into the village, they will burn it down just to feel its warmth.' **African proverb.**

Standards

- The Oxford English Dictionary definition is: **A required or agreed level of quality or attainment.**
- At a personal level people have different standards.
- At a business level agreed standards need to be in place so that everyone understands the level of quality they are expected to attain.
- Examples of standards might include:
    - Dress.
    - Code of behaviour.
    - Customer Service.
- Keep standards simple – easy to understand, easy to put in place and easy to monitor.
- Standards are important - they need to be part of your on going training.
- Don't compromise – there is no point having standards if they are not enforced.
- Make them part of your culture.

'Integrity without knowledge is weak and useless, and knowledge without integrity is dangerous and dreadful.'
Samuel Johnson, English lexicographer.

Process

- The Oxford English Dictionary definition is: **A series of actions or steps towards achieving a particular end.**
- Procedures that define a set a processes by their very nature are a form of control – to make sure things are done properly i.e. to the required standard on a consistent basis.
- The best processes have controls built in:
    - –To stop things happening
    - –To warn you about things about to happen
    - –To tell you when something has happened
- In very simple terms the majority of controls fall into 2 categories:
    - –Preventative: stopping things from going wrong
    - –Detective: identifying things that have or are about to go wrong
- Control reports are a useful tool to monitor what's going on, what's likely to go ' wrong ' what is going wrong.
- Exception reports do exactly that – report on things that look unusual, something that looks out of kilter with the business as usual activity.

Rules

- The Oxford English Dictionary definition is: ***Regulations or principles governing conduct or procedure within a particular area of activity.***
- People need to know the regulations especially those that apply within their area of activity.
- Enforce them (with no exceptions*).
- Make penalties clear.
- People are more likely to follow rules when they understand why they are there.
- Beware of using acronyms, they can cause confusion. If you do want to use them then make sure everyone knows what they mean.
- Make the rules relevant and not too bureaucratic.
- Continually review them to make sure they are still applicable.
- Keep them simple and sensible.

* If you allow exceptions you immediately undermine the importance of your regulations and why you have them in the first place. You also open the door for other people to break the rules.

Rules: discipline

- The Oxford English Dictionary definition is: ***The practice of training people to obey rules or a code of behaviour.***
- Have a code of conduct – this is how you are expected to behave.
- Make sure everyone understands the consequences for not complying with policies, rules, standards and procedures.
- Keep them simple, make them clear – no dubiety.
- Disciplinary procedures serve two purposes:
    - –They act as a warning to prevent people breaking regulations.
    - –They detail the punitive measures that will be taken if it happens.
- Always take action on breaches of discipline without exception.
- Discipline *must* be administered in line with the laid down policy and procedures.
- Disciplinary procedures must work and importantly be seen to work.
- Take action quickly – problems fester and get harder to deal with the longer they are left.
- When you have to punish someone you have not produced the right behaviours from your team. Could you have done anything better?

The •peoplemad success model

Policy

- The Oxford English Dictionary definition is: ***A course or principle of action adopted or proposed by an organisation or individual.***
- There is a need to document and communicate the various policies that an organisation has in place.
- Policies need to be detailed because they have to cover every eventuality especially the legal aspects to make sure there are no loopholes. These include:
    - Health and Safety
    - Human Resources
    - Disciplinary
    - Data Protection
    - IT Security.
- Continually review them to make sure they are still relevant.
- Keep them simple.
- Make them sensible – easy to read and understand.
- Only use legal jargon where absolutely necessary.
- Make them accessible to everyone who is entitled to see them – especially the people who are bound by them and/or have signed to say that they will comply.

The •peoplemad success model

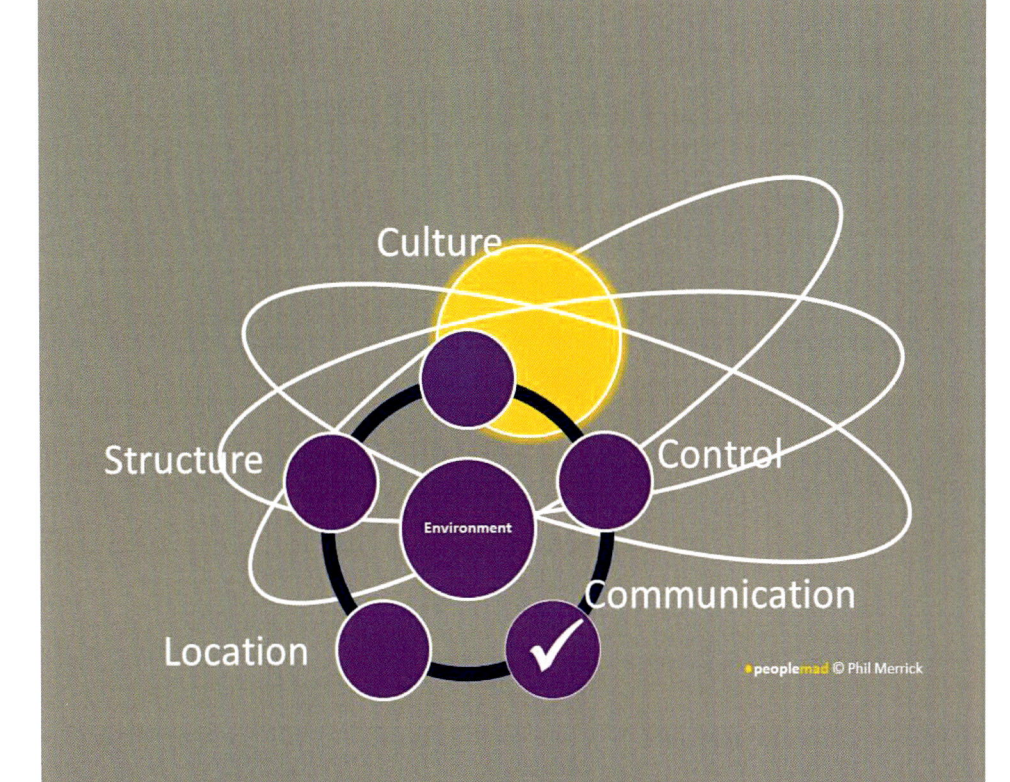

[Diagram: peoplemad success model showing Culture, Structure, Control, Location, Communication around Environment — © Phil Merrick]

Effective communication is critical

Send, receive, understand, ACT

Think OUTCOME

Have a purpose

Think outcome

Think impact

Create a non threatening feedback culture

The •peoplemad success model

Communication

Think OUTCOME

- The Oxford English Dictionary definition is: **The sharing or exchanging of information or ideas.**
- See also 'meetings' - an important part of communication.
- Communication is two ways – sending and receiving.
- Communication should have a purpose – don't do it unless you are absolutely certain why you are doing it.
- If you are the sender it is your job to make sure it is properly received and understood – not the receiver.
- You can blame somebody for not listening but you can't blame someone for not hearing you.
- Before you write something think about the reaction you are trying to stimulate – what do you want the recipient to do? How do you want them to feel?
- Think about your words, think about the impact your communication will have. People are emotional creatures – what emotions will you stir up?
- Make sure people 'get it' – received *and* understood.

Have a purpose to what you say and do
– what outcome do you want?

Communication: meetings

Think OUTCOME

- The Oxford English Dictionary definition is: ***An assembly of people for a purpose, especially for formal discussion.***
- Meetings are key to effective communication.
- **Don't have meetings just for the sake of it.**
- Whilst there can be many types of meetings in the main they fall into 2 categories:
    - –Informal – quick catch up, chat, get things made clear.
    - –Formal – serious issues that need serious attention.
- Be clear about the purpose of the meeting, think *outcome*.
- Only have the right people there (right people, right jobs).
- Some people feel they need to be at meetings just to know what's going on - wrong, unless that's the purpose of the meeting.
- Always appoint a Chairman to run things and someone to take notes/minutes – especially for formal meetings.
- For one to one meetings it is advisable to make notes. If it's a serious matter get both parties to agree them immediately afterwards.
- Have an agenda, stick to the time, keep discussions relevant.
- Meetings can be costly – see next page.

The •peoplemad success model

Meetings are costly when you consider operational down time, the time spent travelling and disruption to the working day. As a discipline, work out the true cost of your meetings: the number of people X (number of hours at the meeting + travel time) X cost per hour + cost of travel for each person. That figure excludes the cost of disrupting the daily routine for each person such as the other work that had to be put on hold while the meeting was taking place. It will scare you. Use technology to save time and money, especially telephone conferencing, webinars, Facetime etc.

'Nothing is more central to an organization's effectiveness than it's ability to transmit accurate, relevant, understandable information among it's members. All the advantages of organizations – economy of scale, financial and technical resources, diverse talents, and contacts – are of no practical value if the organization's members are unaware of what other members require of them and why.'
Saul Gellerman, American author
The management of human resources.

'A good listener is not only popular everywhere, but after a while he knows something.'
Wilson Mizner, playwright.

Communication: feedback

- The Oxford English Dictionary definition is: **Information given in response to a person's performance of a task used as a basis for improvement.**
- Create a non-threatening 'face to face' feedback culture.
- Feedback is good – that's how we learn.
- Feedback should not be taken as personal criticism.
- Feedback needs to be specific on process/behaviour.
- It should be supported by evidence – observation, facts and figures.
- Accepting feedback is difficult if you aren't used to it.
- Action needs to be agreed to improve performance as a result of the feedback.
- There is no such thing as negative feedback if it is delivered properly – it is positive in that ways to make improvements have been identified.
- Give training on giving and accepting feedback.
- Make feedback part of everyday life with your team.

'A little sincerity is a dangerous thing, and a great deal of it is absolutely fatal.'
Oscar Wilde, Irish poet and dramatist.

The •peoplemad success model

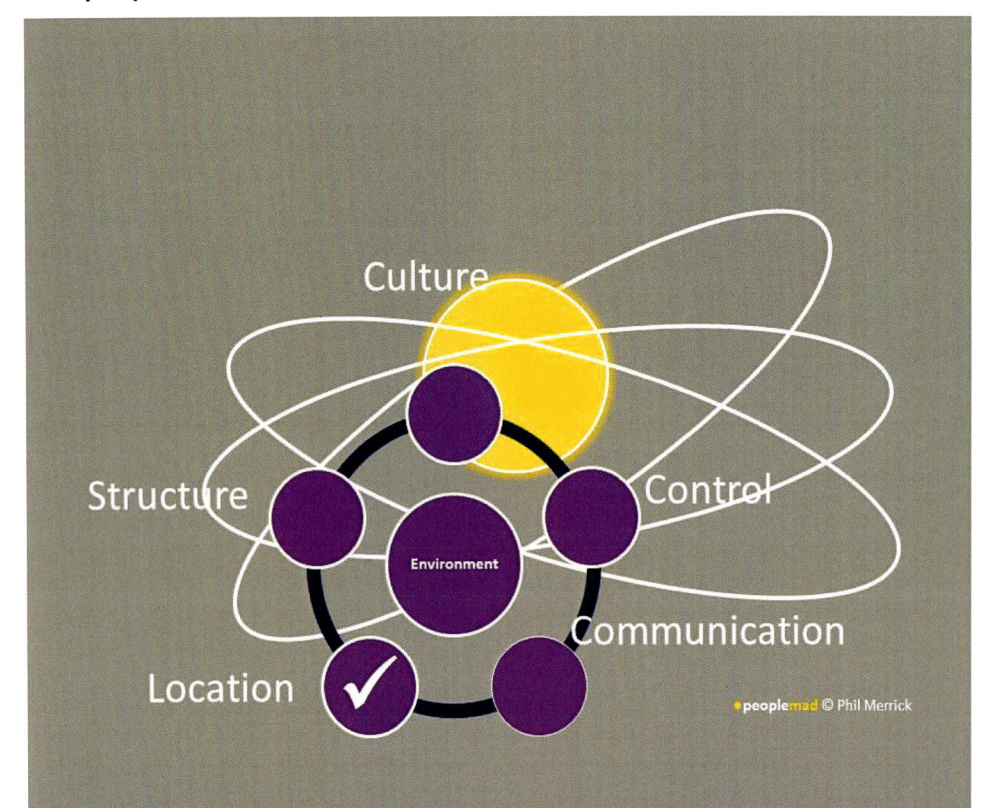

Culture
Structure
Control
Environment
Communication
Location

•peoplemad © Phil Merrick

The best place to be...

Where you live, work, train and practise has a direct impact on your performance

Best conditions
Best performance

The best place to be

- Where you work, train, practise and do your day job has a direct impact on your performance.
- Make the physical working environment a pleasant place to work.
- People like space – cramped conditions aren't conducive to peak performance.
- Decor is important – it doesn't have to be expensive to look nice.
- Lighting needs to be functional not a light show.
- Keep it clean and tidy – tidy space, tidy mind.
- Be mindful of Health and Safety regulations – they are there for a reason.
- The temperature needs to be comfortable.
- Equipment needs to work efficiently and effectively *all the time*.
- When designing the environment think about:
    - The performance of the people using it not the aesthetic qualities of the design.
    - How you want people to communicate (and recognise that sometimes people need privacy).
- In sport, creating the right physical environment with the right facilities is critical in improving the performance of young sports people.

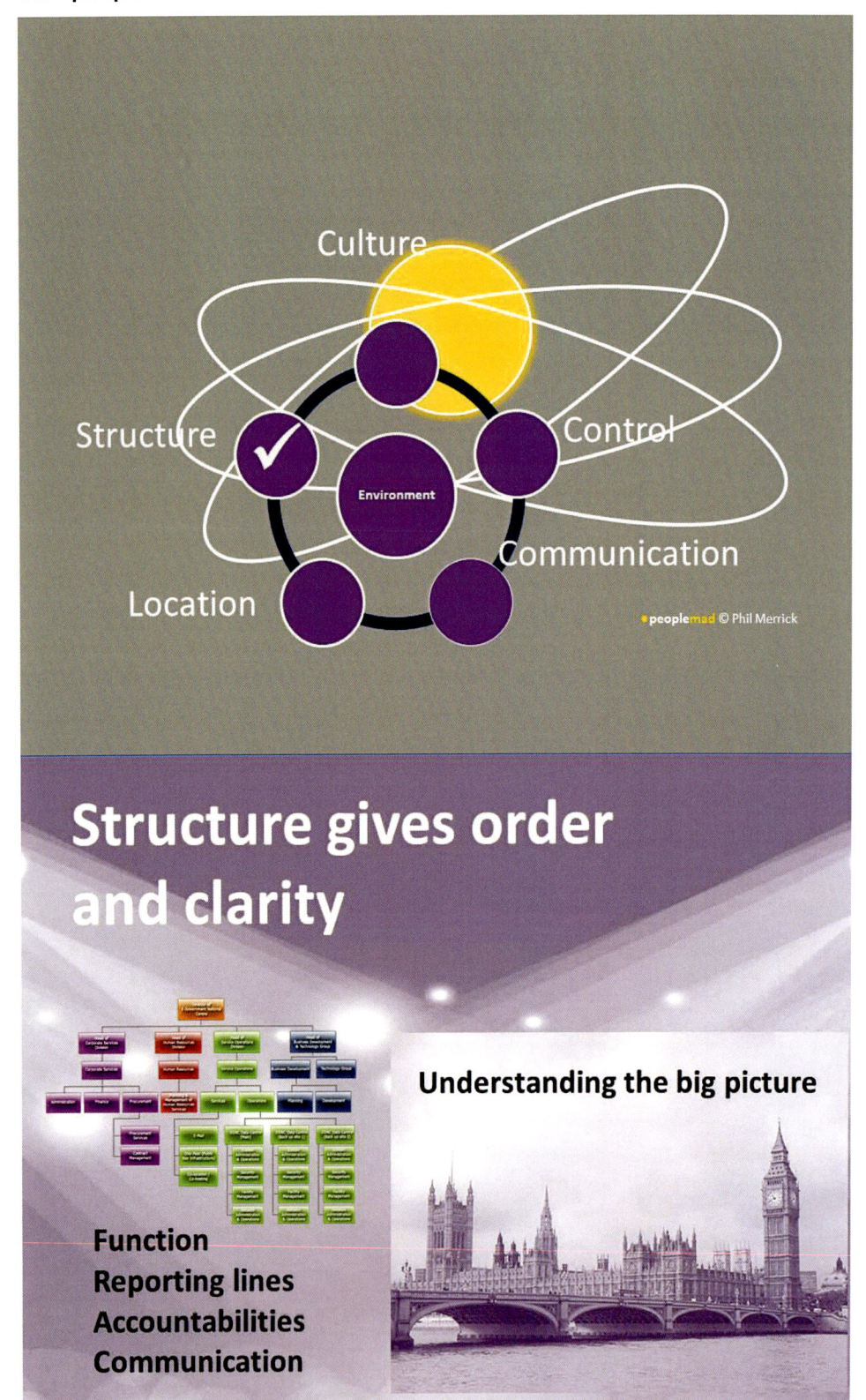

The •peoplemad success model

Culture
Structure ✓
Control
Environment
Communication
Location

•peoplemad © Phil Merrick

Structure gives order and clarity

Understanding the big picture

Function
Reporting lines
Accountabilities
Communication

Structure

- Structure is the organisational design and the operating structure within which people go about doing their daily work.
- The right structure is important for a number of reasons, including:
    - Clarity of functions – what happens where
    - Clarity of reporting lines – who reports to whom
    - Clarity of accountabilities – who is responsible for what
    - The understanding of your role in the bigger picture
    - Effective communication up, down and across the structure
- This applies at every level – organisations, divisions, businesses, teams.
- In your teams it is important to know who is responsible for what, who reports to whom and your role in the team.
- Have a look at how other businesses are structured. By product? By geography? Look at a global business (such as a car manufacturer) to really understand the importance of getting the structure right. These structures are driven by market forces – where is the best place to locate this particular part of my business?

Leadership tips

- Lead by example and encourage others to do the same.
- Encourage communication, collaboration and co-operation.
- Continually review all policies and procedures to make sure they are appropriate and in line with changing conditions.
- Don't feel guilty about administering disciplinary action:
    - people shouldn't break the rules.
    - you can't make exceptions.
- Keep administration to an absolute minimum.
- Encourage focus, minimise distraction and interruption.
- Talk to people, ask questions, get involved.
- Make people feel part of what is going on.
- Most people like structure and order – link this to purpose and you have a strong foundation on which to build your team.
- People perform better when they feel good about themselves so it is important that they know their role and feel that they are contributing to the bigger picture.
- Celebrate success.

The •peoplemad success model

Create the right environment

Culture
Location
Control
Environment
Communication
Structure

•peoplemad © Phil Merrick

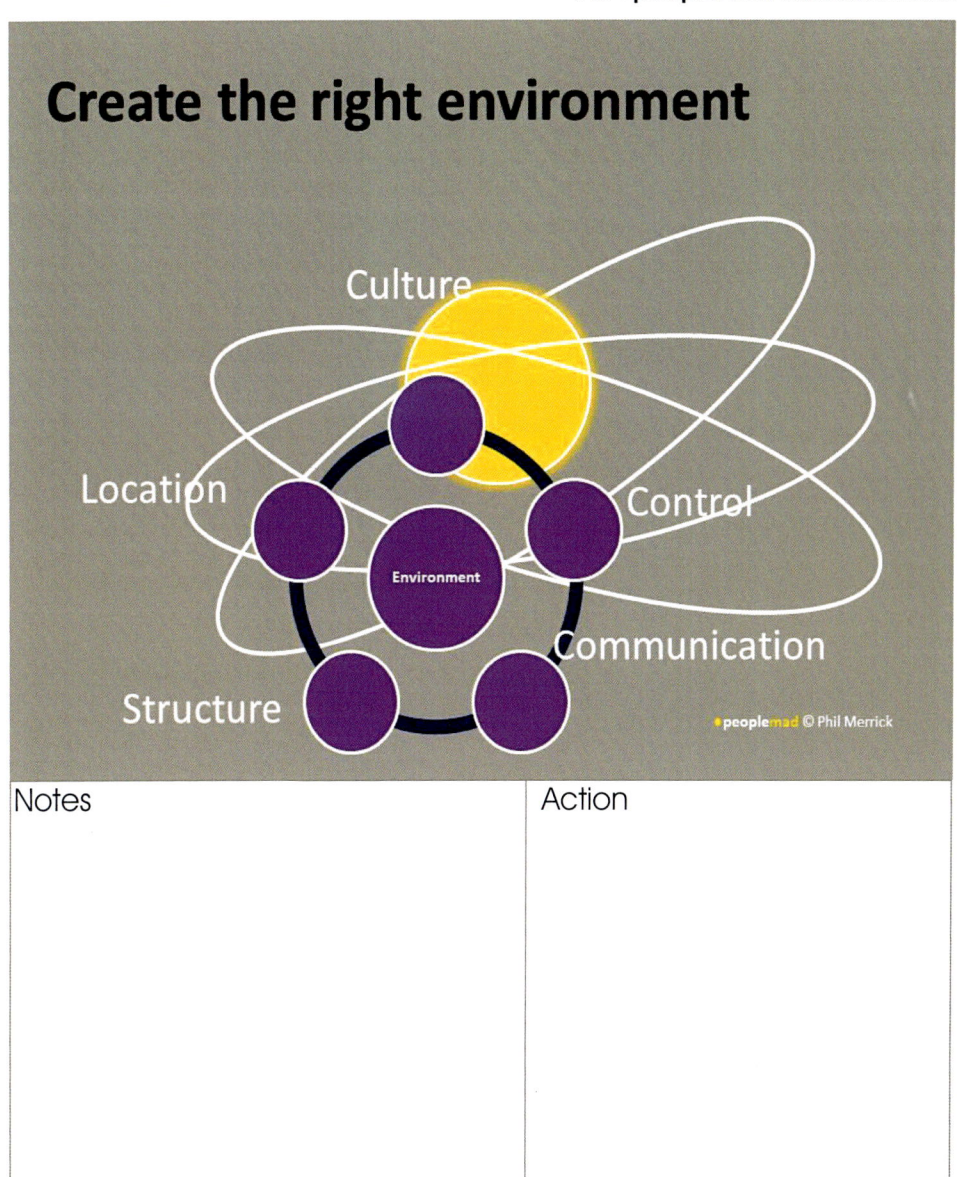

Notes	Action

Your own •**peoplemad** notes

7. Build your own capability

In this section:
- The •**peoplemad** success model
- Take ownership of your career
- Your career ladder
- Be careful you don't fall
- Your life is in your hands
- Follow the •**peoplemad** rules for your own performance
- Use the •**peoplemad** planets for your own performance
- Develop your game plan
- Clarify your vision
- Devise your strategy
- What motivates you?
- Carry out self analysis
- Today versus Tomorrow – some example questions
- Today versus Tomorrow – some ideas
- Set some objectives
- Develop a plan
- Simple planning
- Develop your competencies
- Competencies
- Get the right attitude

Build your own capability continued

In this section continued:

- Positive attitude
- Never mention 'failure'
- Winning mentality
- Winning mentality: making actions count
- Work ethic
- Influence
- Being influenced
- Influencing others
- Don't waste time trying to influence…
- A word of caution…
- Strengthen your ability
- Work hard, play hard
- Build your support team
- Establish a support structure
- Performing on the day
- Attain peak performance
- Some important rules
- How do you want people to see you?
- Create the right image
- Your personal action plan
- Your own •peoplemad notes

The •peoplemad success model

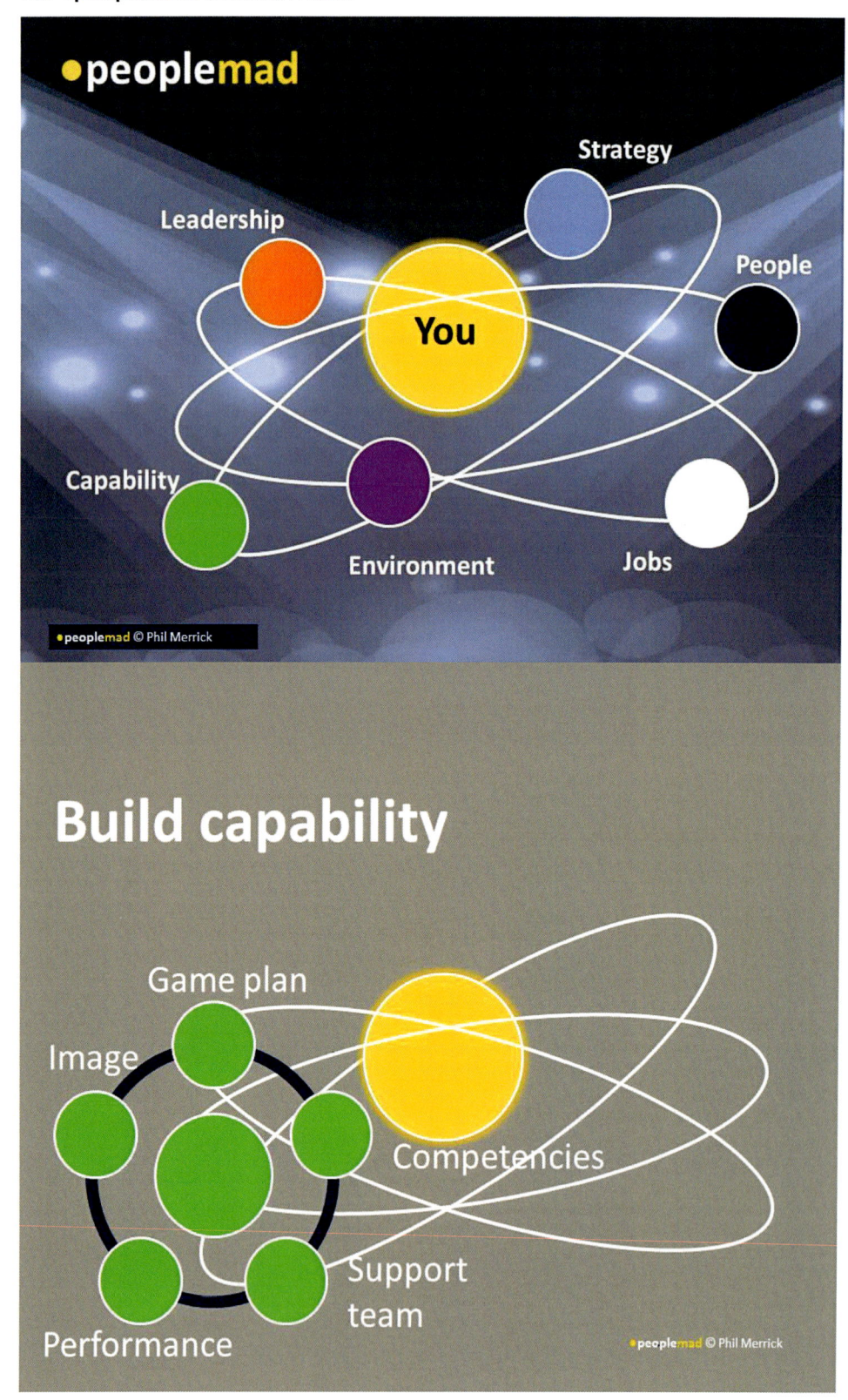

•peoplemad

- Strategy
- Leadership
- People
- You
- Capability
- Environment
- Jobs

•peoplemad © Phil Merrick

Build capability

- Game plan
- Image
- Competencies
- Support team
- Performance

•peoplemad © Phil Merrick

Okay let's move on to capability. This is about you – you trying to be the best, improving your own individual performance.

Obviously it helps your own development but if you are part of a team then their overall performance will be enhanced as well and you of course need to lead by example. We can always learn new things – •**peoplemad** is about being the best and quite simply you won't be the best without working hard and doing absolutely everything you can to improve from where you are today.

Matthew Syed, International table tennis champion said in his book 'Bounce':

'The differences between expert performers and normal adults reflect a life-long persistence of deliberate effort to improve performance.'

A life long persistence of deliberate effort.

I too believe that success comes from hard work and a unique set of circumstances, which you can create for yourself.

Do you have a vision? Is it clear? Are you excited by it? Are you passionate about it?

The •peoplemad success model

One of the issues for young adults is that they don't know what to do with their lives so this model helps them with their career as well as giving them a grounding in sound business principles.

Have ambition and a plan be the best you can.

So what do I need to do to improve?
How do I get from my performance today to my better performance tomorrow?
What skills do I need?
You will be good at something if you:
- Have the best coach/teacher/mentor (i.e. the best support team; remember surround yourself with the right people)
- Learn the right technique
- Work hard
- Believe in yourself
- Yearn to be the best you can be
- Practise, practise, practise
- Don't give up.

And what about image? We've all got an image, how other people see us – is it how I want to be seen? What does my image need to be?
Remember people deal with people they like dealing with.

What about my performance, how I perform on the day? Whether it's playing the 18th hole at Augusta or teaching a class of students, the principles of peak performance are exactly the same.
Stay in the zone, don't reflect on mistakes, the missed putt, the missed penalty, forgetting your lines – and don't look too far ahead… What if this? What if that?
Keep all your thoughts on the present, in the present.

The now is all there is. Get that right and the future takes care of itself.

Success means different things to different people. You need to understand what drives you, what makes you happy. How do you define your own success? We all want different things.
Give yourself the advantage – do something better than everybody else. Watch other people who already have that skill. Do things. Read things. Learn things. Get interested in different things. Ask questions. Be more interested in other people than you are in yourself.

'*While you're talking about yourself you are not learning anything.*' **Phil Merrick.**

The •peoplemad success model

Take ownership of your career

- Whether working as part of a team or performing on your own, take ownership of your career and personal development.

- Clarify your vision.
- Devise your strategy.
- Carry out self analysis – today versus tomorrow.
- Set some objectives.
- Develop a plan.
- Get the right attitude.
- Build your capability.
- Establish a support structure.
- Create the right image.
- Attain peak performance.

'To accomplish great things we must not only act, but also dream; not only plan, but also believe.' **Anatole France, French writer.**

The ●peoplemad success model

Your career ladder

Using the career ladder analogy is a great way to put your career in perspective.
- How long is your ladder?
- Does it reach as high as you want it to?
- Do you know which rung you are on?
- How steep is it?
- How difficult is it to climb to the top?
- Is your ladder safe?
- Is someone 'footing' (securing) your ladder or trying to knock you off?

- **Are you on the right ladder?**

At some point you might want to change your job/career. There is nothing wrong with stepping off a higher rung of one ladder onto the lower rung of another if it is a longer ladder.

The •**peoplemad** success model

Be careful you don't fall

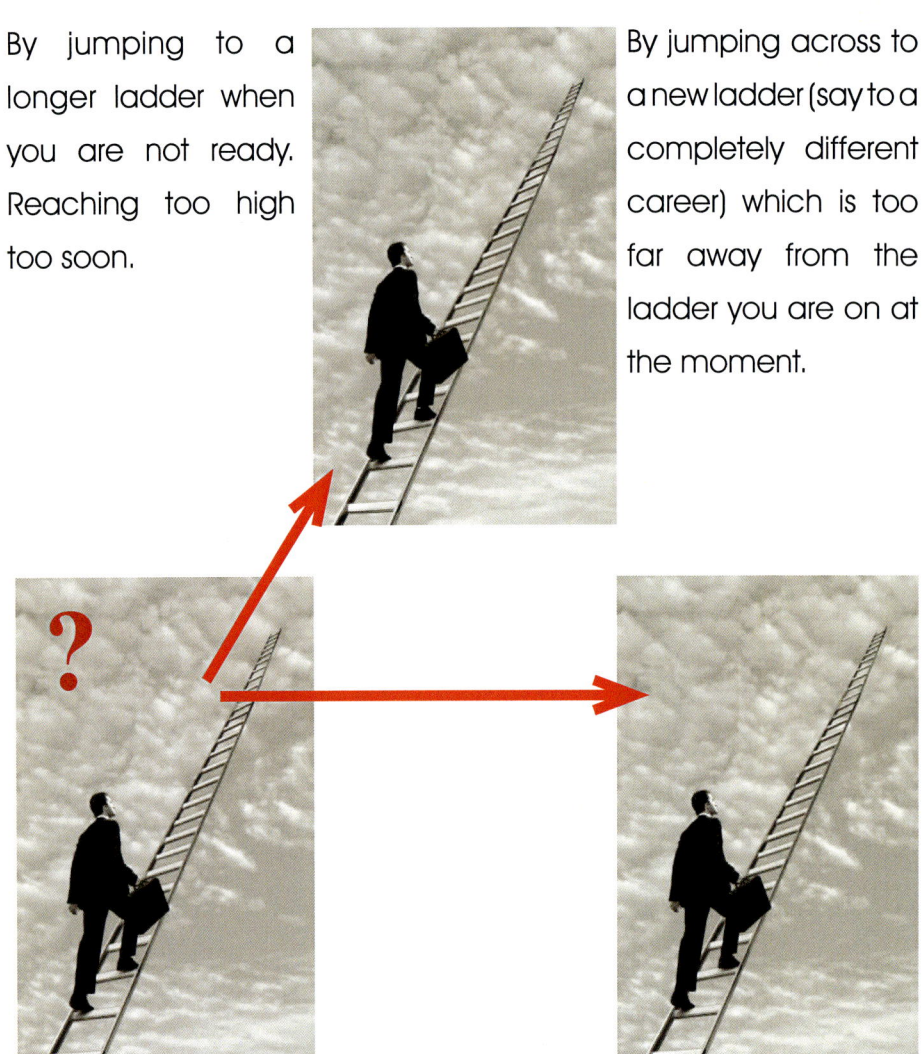

By jumping to a longer ladder when you are not ready. Reaching too high too soon.

By jumping across to a new ladder (say to a completely different career) which is too far away from the ladder you are on at the moment.

The more closely aligned your new career ladder is to your old one, the easier it will be to step across.

The •peoplemad success model

Your life is in your hands

Think OUTCOME

- You can achieve whatever you want providing you believe it's possible.

- Take ownership
    - Don't complain.
    - Don't make excuses.
    - Don't blame other people.
    - Don't put up barriers.

- If things aren't working out, do something about it.

- You need to get the best people on your side:
    - believe in the •**peoplemad** rules.

- The only thing stopping you from achieving success is you – believe in yourself.

- It's your life – get on with it and make things happen.

'It is never too late to be what you might have been.'
George Eliot, English novelist.

The **•peoplemad** success model

Follow the **•peoplemad** rules for your own performance

1. Believe in yourself
2. Surround yourself with the right people
3. Keep it simple

'Luck has nothing to do with it, because I have spent many, many hours, countless hours, on the court working for my one moment in time, not knowing when it would come.'
Serena Williams, American Tennis champion.

'Genius is nothing but labour and diligence.'
William Hogarth, English painter and caricaturist.

Do everything you can to feel good about yourself.

Use the •peoplemad planets for your own performance

Use the 6 planets as the key parts of your methodology:
- Develop your strategy.
- Surround yourself with the right people.
- Get the right people doing the right things.
- Create the right environment.
- Build your own capability.
- Display leadership.

In very simple terms:
- Know what you're aiming to achieve and get the right people on board.
- Get them doing the right things in an environment that will allow them to flourish and perform at their very best.
- Build your own capability and display strong leadership at all times.

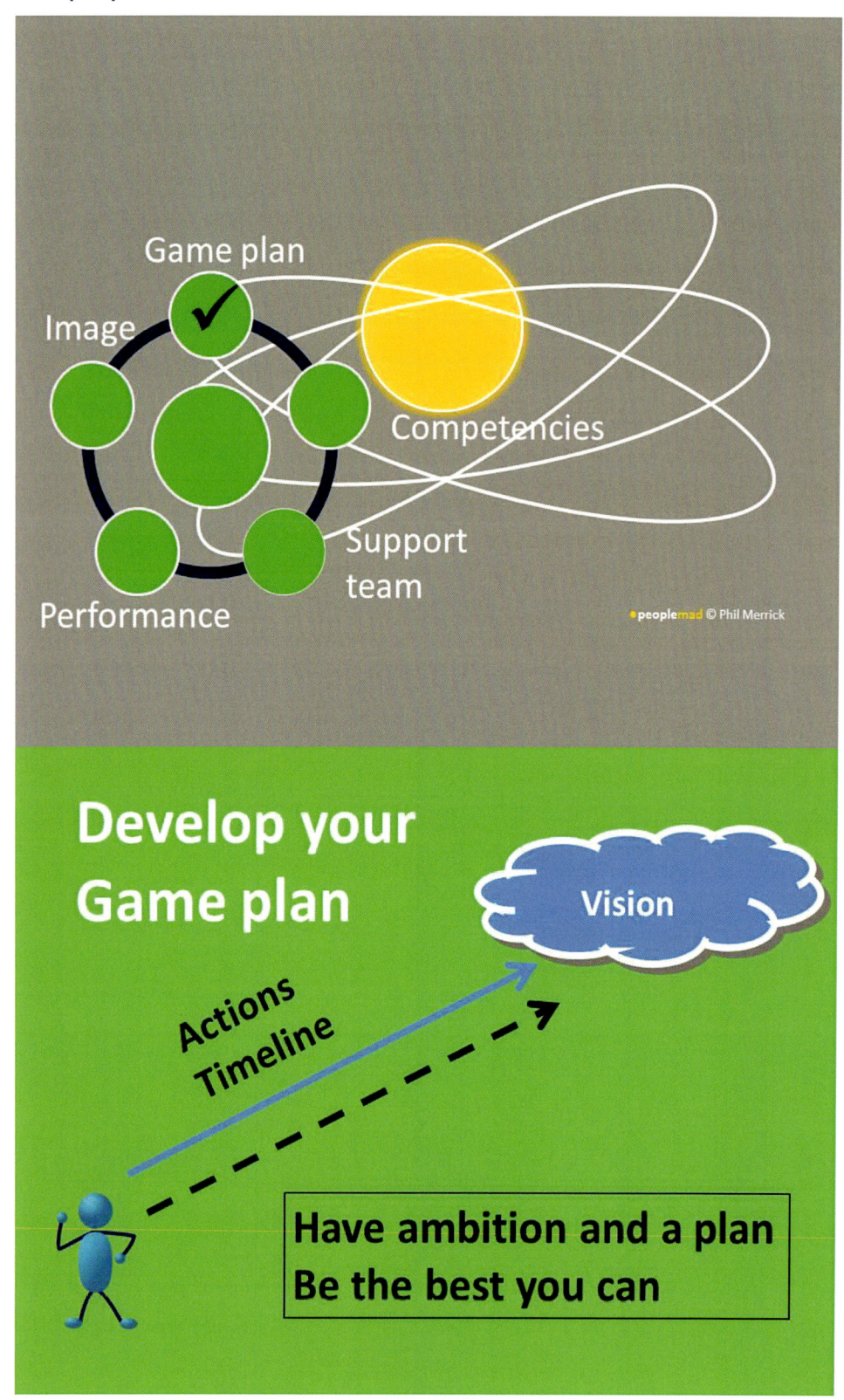

The ●peoplemad success model

Game plan ✓
Image
Competencies
Support team
Performance

●peoplemad © Phil Merrick

Develop your Game plan

Vision

Actions Timeline

**Have ambition and a plan
Be the best you can**

Clarify your vision

- Aspire, desire, dream.
- Open your mind.
- Don't put restrictions on your thoughts.
- Believe you can do anything that's physically possible.
- Research it.
- Draw it, paint it, write it down.
- Give it as much detail as possible.
- Sleep on it.
- Close your eyes and paint it in your mind.

Check and rationalise –

- Are you passionate about it?
- Can you get excited by it?
- Is it within reach? It doesn't have to be easy but it needs to feel achievable to keep motivated.

Think OUTCOME

> What would you do if you knew you couldn't fail?
> What would you do if you didn't care what people think?

The •peoplemad success model

Think it
See it
Draw it
Write it
Want it

Vision

Believe it

Don't lose sight of it

'Without a vision we perish. If you don't have something to lead you on then there's nowhere to go; the journey finishes.'
Jonathan Edwards, 2000 Olympics Gold Medallist.

Devise your strategy

The simplest definition of strategy is:

Knowing where you are today, knowing where you want to be tomorrow and having a plan to get there.

Knowing where you are today:
- Carry out a review – a self analysis (see next pages).
- Understand you and how you feel about things.
- Understand your life, your career and where you are today in as much detail as possible.
- Assess everything – including other people in your life.
- Be truthful to yourself as to the realistic position.
- The more honest and accurate the information the easier it will be to plan.

Think OUTCOME

'If you have a goal or anything you want to achieve in life, don't let anybody get in your way because you can do it and there are so many people and things that will feel like they're trying to set you back – but honestly find the path that you want to take in life and follow it and stick to it because if I can do it, I'm a normal girl, anybody can do anything they want to do.'
Samantha Murray, 2012 Olympics Silver Medallist.

The •peoplemad success model

Knowing where you want to be tomorrow:
- Start with your vision.
- Take your thoughts and drawings and turn them into detailed descriptions of what the future looks like.
- Think of everything especially the people you would like to get involved to help you.

Develop a strategy:
- Plot how to move from today's position to the described vision – prioritise and plan.
- Be creative.
- Don't put up barriers.
- Get other people involved especially those that will be working with you or impacted by your strategy.
- Get buy in and support as early as possible.
- Assess the risks and put mitigating plans in place.

'All the things we achieve are things we have first of all imagined.'
David Malouf, Australian writer.

What motivates you?

- Money?
- Enjoyment?
- Pride in the job?
- Helping others?
- Is your motivation intrinsic? e.g. feeling good.
- Is your motivation extrinsic? e.g. trophies and glory.
- Remember you'll be better at something if you enjoy doing it.

Picture your ideal day
- Travelling or based at home?
- Office based or out and about?
- Working alone or mixing with people?
- What do you see yourself doing when you wake up in the morning?

'You can do or be whatever you want in your own life. Nothing can stop you, except your own fears. Don't blame anyone else... you have the power to make the decision. Just do it.'
Nola Diamantopoulos, Greek-Australian creative workshop tutor.

The •**peoplemad** success model

Carry out self analysis

- Describe how you see yourself today in as much detail as possible:
    - –Give your own view.
    - –Get a friends view.
    - –Get a relative's view.
- Describe how you see yourself tomorrow in as much detail as possible:
    - –Be creative.
    - –Be realistic.
    - –Don't put up barriers.
- Carry out a gap analysis between the present and future state:
    - –Where are the main differences?
    - –Do you understand why?
    - –Identify where you want to make changes.
    - –Think about the risks of making the changes.
    - –Think about the risks of not making the changes.
- Prioritise your actions and create a plan.

The •peoplemad success model

Today v Tomorrow

Vision

Where you want to be tomorrow

Where you are today

**Carry out a self analysis
What motivates you?
What do you need to change?**

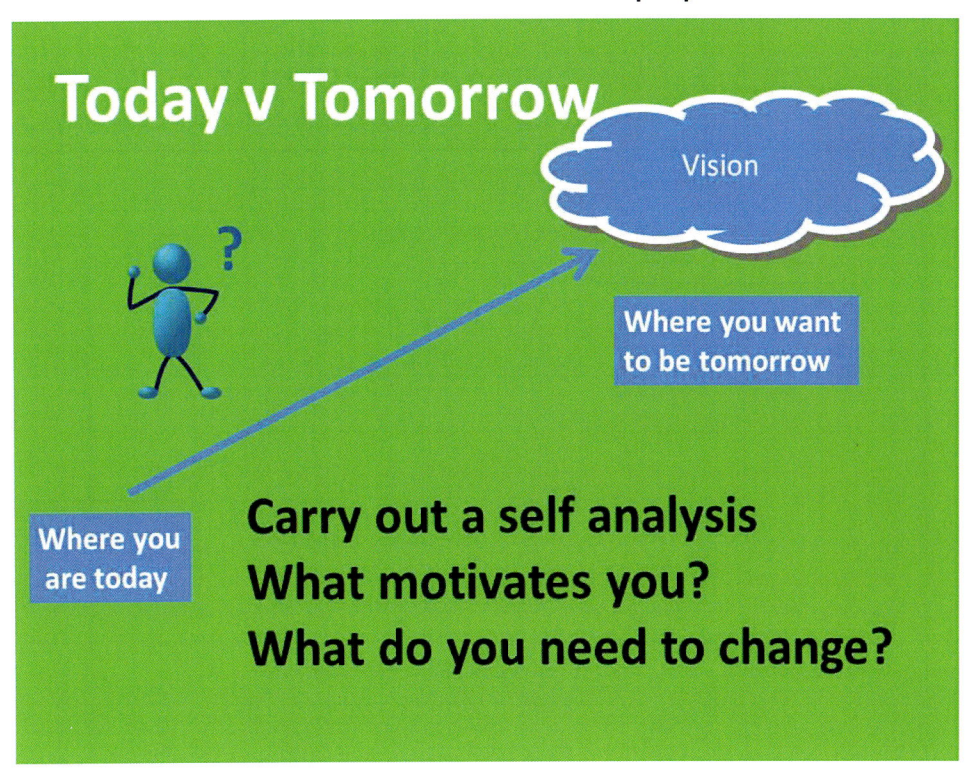

Over 35,000 people run in the London Marathon every year knowing that they aren't going to win. So they must be motivated by something other than winning. Raising money for charity, the fun, the sense of achievement?

When he reached number one in the World golf rankings Rory McIlroy said his motivation was just to be better than everyone else. Brilliant.

What drives you? What excites you? What is important to you?

The •peoplemad success model

Today versus Tomorrow
some example questions

- What motivates you?
- What do you like about yourself?
- What do you dislike about yourself?
- What makes you happy?
- Anything you feel strongly about?
- What upsets you?
- What annoys you?
- Who inspires you?
- If you could change one thing?
- Unfulfilled dreams?
- What do you like doing?
- What do you think about?
- How do you spend your day?
- Are you an introvert or an extrovert?
- Are you a fashion leader or follower?
- What do you worry about?

> You need ambition, something to aim for, something to get you excited about the future.

Today versus Tomorrow
some ideas

- Skills
- Knowledge
- Experience
- Good at?
- Bad at?
- Beliefs
- People
- Music
- Hobbies
- Emotions
- Fashion
- Friends
- Family
- Image
- Views
- Religion
- Home
- Work
- Travel
- Character
- Bad habits
- Food
- Fitness
- Charities
- Phobias
- Worries & concerns

'I believe that we are solely responsible for our choices, and we have to accept the consequences of every deed, word and thought throughout our lifetime.'

Elizabeth Kubler-Ross, psychiatrist.

The •peoplemad success model

Set some objectives

Think OUTCOME

- You now have a vision and a strategy – objectives will give focus to make it happen.
- When you describe your vision then you need to attach some objectives that will make you achieve it.
- Keep them simple.
- Make sure they are the right ones and lead you down the right path.
- Describe them in such a way that there is no doubt when they are achieved.
- Set some short term objectives – they will act as stepping stones and give a sense of achievement along the way.
- Get buy in – think about everyone who is impacted by your actions.
- Communicate progress.
- Celebrate success when they are achieved.

'Life isn't about finding yourself. Life is about creating yourself.'
George Bernard Shaw, Irish playwright.

The •peoplemad success model

Personal objectives

4

3

2

1

Your target

Your personal journey

Have ambition and a plan.
Be the best you can.

The **•peoplemad** success model

Develop a plan

- A simple plan is a list of what your are going to do and when.

- The more challenging your goals, the more complicated the change being undertaken and the more people you need to involve then the more detailed your plan will need to be.

- Some activity will depend on other things that need to be done first – in project management land these are called dependencies.

- Think of the risks involved – they will need to be managed and they take time.

- Think of the people involved – they will need to be managed and they take time ☺.

- Plans need to be kept up to date and communicated to whoever needs to be kept informed.

- Planning is a skill get good at it. Make personal planning a habit.

Simple planning

- Make a list of all the things that need to be done.
- Put them in some sort of order remembering that some things might be dependent on others (e.g. if you are building a house the walls can't be built until the foundations are in).
- Draw a timeline and put the actions that need to be taken under the appropriate dates.
- A trick is to start with the end date and work backwards (like planning a journey – what time do I want to get there? How long will it take? So what time do I need to leave?).
- Put in some milestones – where you want to be by a certain point in time. This will help target progress and give a sense of continual achievement.
- Sit back and assess whether your plan is realistic and achievable under your timescales.
- Have I missed anything?
- What would happen if?
- Plan, plan and plan again until you are happy.

The •peoplemad success model

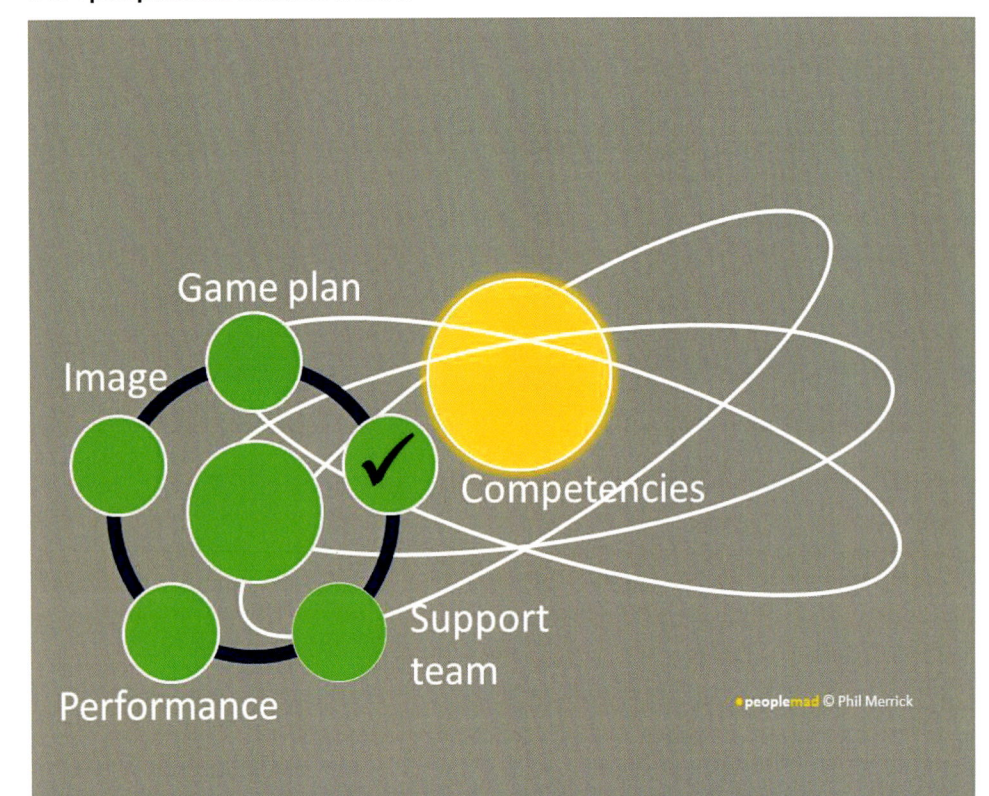

Game plan
Image
Competencies
Support team
Performance

•peoplemad © Phil Merrick

Develop your competencies

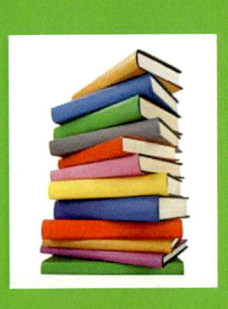

Attitude
Influence
Talent
Skill
Knowledge
Experience

Dealing with other people

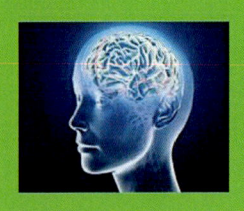

Competencies

- The Oxford English Dictionary definition is: **Having the necessary ability or knowledge to do something successfully.**

- The trick is in how this ability and knowledge is applied.

    –Attitude: Settled way of thinking or feeling
    –Talent: Natural aptitude or skill.
    –Skill: The ability to do something well.
    –Knowledge: Information and skills acquired through experience and education.

- Competence is not finite – your attitude, talent, skill and knowledge are all areas that can be continually improved through effort.

'Never set limits, go after your dreams, don't be afraid to push the boundaries, and laugh a lot, it's good for you!'
Paula Radcliffe MBE, World record beating long distance runner.

The •peoplemad success model

Get the right attitude

- **Be a winner:**
    - Work hard.
    - Be the vision; be that person today.
    - Display leadership:
        - Listen.
        - Inspire.
        - Make decisions.
        - Show respect.
- **Be confident:**
    - Solid eye contact.
    - Of course I can.
        - I am the star of my own show.
        - I am taking this space.
- **Be in control:**
    - Rise above everything.
        - Choose what you want to believe and hear.
    - Feel interested not threatened.
        - 'what makes you say that?'
    - Stay in adult state.
        - Be the parent not the child.
    - Influence don't be influenced.
        - Be the Conductor of your orchestra.

The •peoplemad success model

Positive attitude

- Success comes from 100% belief.
- The body does what it is told by the brain.
- 70,000 thoughts a day (so they say) – don't waste them.
- Don't talk about failure.
- Don't even think about failure.
- Believe, make it happen.
- Moaning adds no value whatsoever.
- If you don't like it do something about it.
- Don't worry about things you can do nothing about.
- Don't worry about people who do not affect your World.
- Negativity is draining.
- Look forward – get excited.

'They are able because they think they are able.'
Virgil, Roman poet.

'Make the best of every situation – whether good bad or indifferent.'
Phil Merrick.

Never mention 'failure'

- Don't talk about failure.
- The word does not have a place in the **•peoplemad** vocabulary.
- We don't fail we try different things.
- If something doesn't come off we learn from it and do it differently next time.
- Stretching yourself and pushing the boundaries inevitably means that everything you try will not work out.
- That's how you discover things.
- How do you know how good you could be if you don't reach the point where you don't succeed.
- If you believe you will achieve your goals at some point in the future and accept that you will have setbacks along the way, then each set back is one step closer to achieving those goals.
- Don't be afraid of making mistakes.
- Push, try, learn, push, try, learn…

'Life is trying things to see if they work.'
Ray Bradbury, American author.

The **•peoplemad** success model

Lose the word 'failure'

**Stretch boundaries
Try different things
Raise the bar**

A good analogy is the pole vault where they raise the bar to a new height every time you clear it. If you keep raising the bar at some point you will knock it off. This is not failure, this is seeing how high you can go.

'If at first you don't succeed, try, try again.'
William Edward Hickson, writer.

'If at first you do succeed, try something harder.'
Ann Landers, American advice columnist.

The •peoplemad success model

Winning mentality

- The Oxford English Dictionary definition is:
    - **–Winner: a person or thing that wins.**
    - **–Mentality: characteristic way of thinking.**
- Winning people have winning ways – they know what's needed to be a winner.
- Winners inspire other people to be winners.
- Winners are positive people – they don't think about failure.
- Winners usually have high energy levels and a desire to get things done.
- Winners who have tasted success want more of it.
- Winners hate losing – 'show me a good loser and I'll show you a loser'.
- Be a winner, surround yourself with winners.

'I don't train to come second.'
Michael Jamieson, Scottish 200 metres breast stroke swimmer after getting a silver medal in the 2014 Glasgow Commonwealth Games. He was the games' pin up boy and favourite for the gold.

The •**peoplemad** success model

Winning mentality: making actions count

- Try to make *all* your actions count.
- Think about why you are doing something.
- Always aim to have a positive OUTCOME.
- If it's worth doing it's worth doing properly.
- What OUTCOME do you want?
- Does it move you nearer towards your goals?
- Often your desired OUTCOME will be determined by a series of actions; if one isn't carried out properly then this could affect the benefits of the others. They could even be completely wasted.
- Focus on them all – they all count.
- Concentrate to the end – be relentless.

In golf the last short putt is as important as the 250 yard drive off the tee.

To be a good singer you need to hit every single note.

Footballers have to deliver the final pass. All the previous good passes count for nothing when there is a shot off-target, a missed penalty, a bad cross – wasted effort that makes all the previous actions wasted effort as well.

The best performers know how to complete the job properly – concentrate, focus on the task, deliver.

The •peoplemad success model

Work ethic

- The Oxford English Dictionary definition is:
    - **Work: activity involving mental or physical effort done in order to achieve a result**
    - **Ethic: set of moral principles.**

- People with a strong work ethic believe that working hard is the right thing to do – it is one of their values.

- Talent alone is not enough – success needs hard work.

- Skills have to be learnt – they only improve with practise, practise and more practise.

- Successful people are not afraid of hard work.

- The 'work smarter not harder' saying should be 'work smarter and harder'.

- Make hard work a value for you and your team.

- Caution 'All work no play' is dangerous. It is important for people to find the right work/life balance that works for their own personal circumstances (see Work hard, play hard).

Influence

- The Oxford English Dictionary definition is: **The capacity to have an effect on the character or behaviour on someone or something.**

How good are you at influencing the way other people think?

'Every day your life is affected by thousands of decisions and actions taken by other people including politicians, employers, employees, friends, relatives, suppliers etc. etc. How well they perform directly influences your success and happiness.
How much influence do you have over their performance? Take control.'
Phil Merrick.

'Influence those who influence others.'
John Fairchild, American publisher.

The •peoplemad success model

Influence

Think OUTCOME

Do you influence other people?

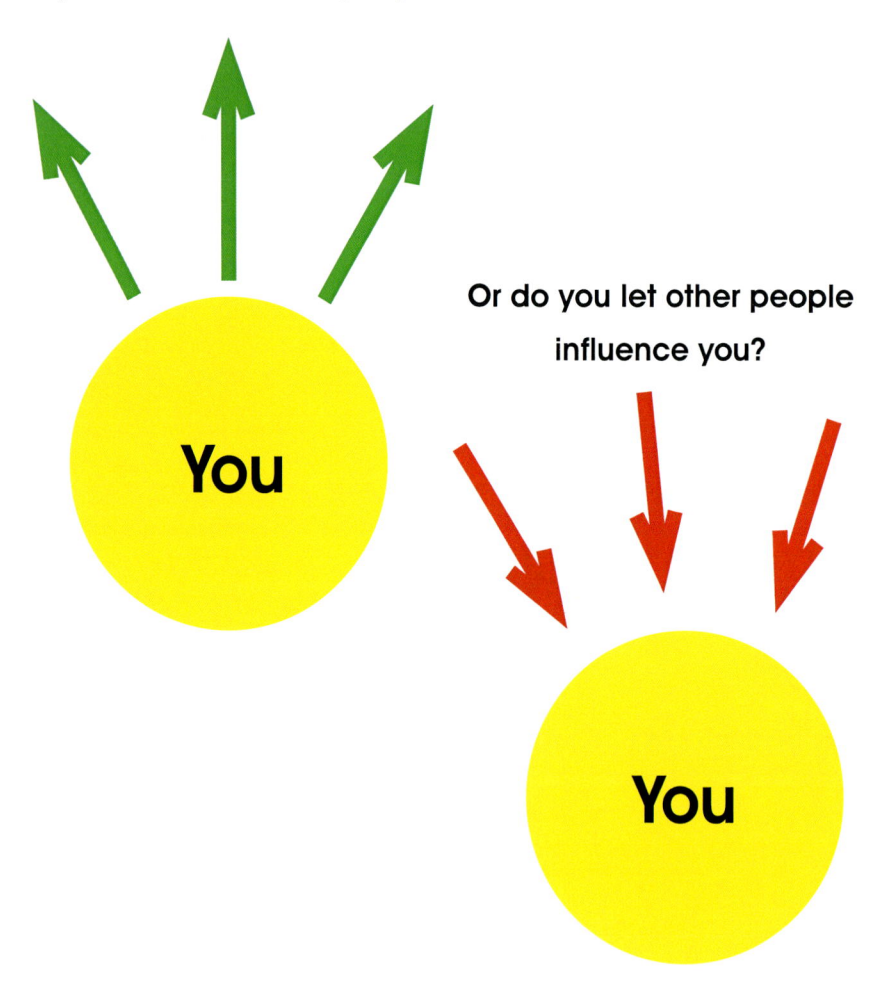

You

Or do you let other people influence you?

You

Being Influenced

- You control your thoughts so you decide whether you want to listen to what other people have to say.
- Build your knowledge. This will help you challenge what you are told and you can make up your own mind.
- Think of the source. Is it credible? Do they know what they are talking about?

Here are some simple techniques to stop you being influenced by the wrong people and shield you from hurtful words:

- Think of the words as arrows, put a mental shield around you so that the arrows bounce off without getting through.
- They are just words – If they were uttered in a foreign language you wouldn't understand them anyway.
- Rise above it. Tell yourself that the words don't actually matter. You know what you are doing; dismiss it as if they don't know what they are talking about.

The important point here is that you listen to credible sources, consider the points and decide whether or not you want to be influenced. You stay in control.

At any point in time there are people in your life who are influencing the level of your success. Make sure you know who they are. Make sure the influence is positive.

The •peoplemad success model

Influencing others

- Build your knowledge. This will help you influence what other people think.

- There will be some people who are adamant that they don't agree with you. Accept it and move on. Don't waste precious time on them. It is difficult changing someone's attitude towards something if they have strong beliefs.

- Don't waste time trying to influence the wrong people. Work out the people who you want in your world and spend your time with them.

- Use the analogy of heading off on a journey and getting people on your bus, all heading in the same direction.

- There will be those people wanting to get on your bus, those thinking about getting on the bus and those who don't want to join you on your journey.

- Concentrate only on the people already on the bus and those thinking of getting on.

- The very important people in your life are the ones on the bus – look after them.

The •**peoplemad** success model

● **Don't waste time trying to influence the wrong people**

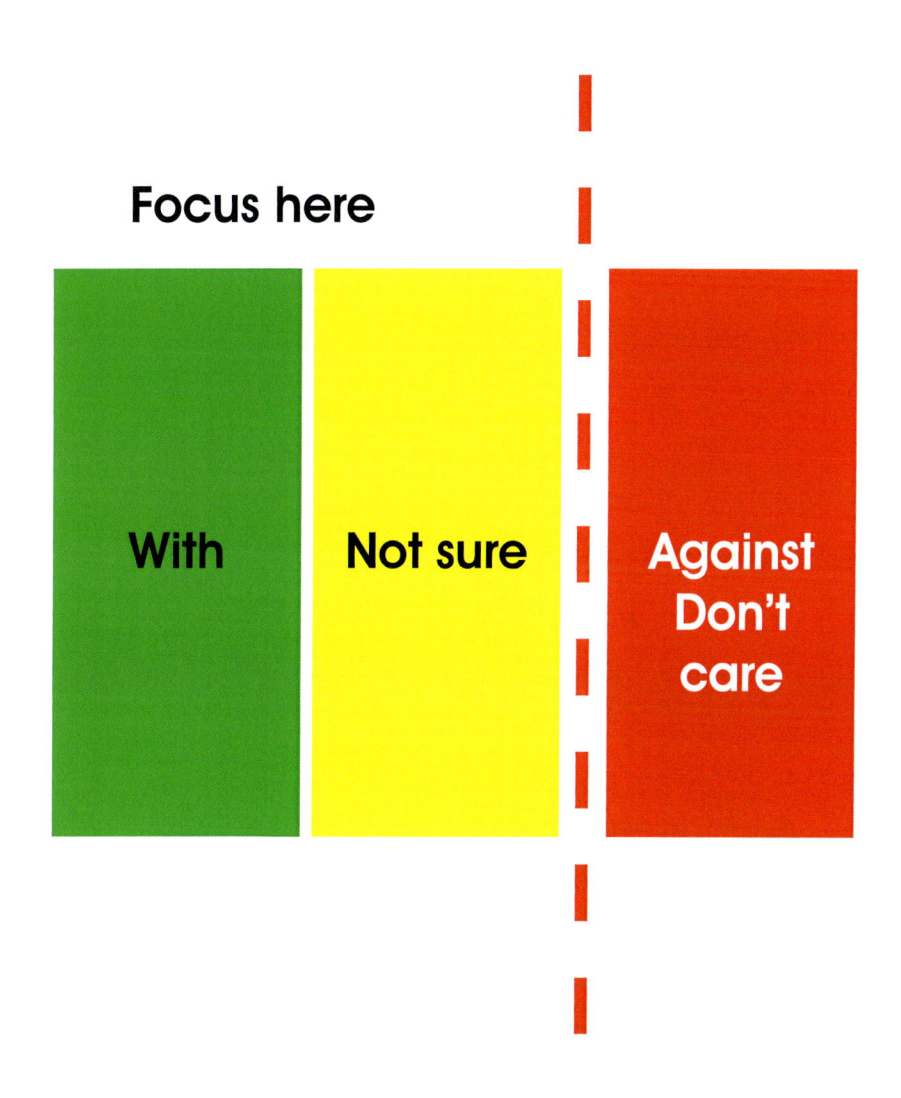

Focus here

| With | Not sure | Against Don't care |

The •peoplemad success model

A word of caution...

- Your success is affected by the actions of other people:
    - people working with you.
    - AND people working against you.
- People working against you will include competitors, adversaries and those who don't agree with what you are trying to do.
- People working against you will have their own reasons for not supporting you.
- Remember it is not easy to change someone's beliefs.
- Do not waste time on difficult people.
- Solicit support from people who are already on side or are willing to listen.
- Focus your efforts on the people working with you.
- Refer to Section 8 – Dealing with opposition.
- Remember – surround yourself with the right people.

'I don't know the secret to success but I know the secret to failure – and that's trying to keep everyone happy.'
Mark Sheehan, guitarist. The Script. September 2014.

Strengthen your ability

- Develop your people skills:
    - How to manage other people.
    - How to manage yourself.
- Develop core skills:
    - Talent.
    - Technique.
    - Practise, practise, practise.
- Improve your knowledge:
    - Job in hand.
    - Competition.
    - Watch and learn from other people – find a role model.
- Get as much experience as you can:
    - Make it targeted, have a plan.
- Get your fitness levels up to the required standard:
    - Physical and mental.
- Build your communication skills:
    - Actively listen.
    - Get interested in people.
- Push the boundaries:
    - Stretch the comfort zone, try new things.

Work hard, play hard

- Peak performance is not achieved through non stop working.

- You need rest and the right intake of food and water so that your energy levels are at their highest when you need them.

- It is important to have a release. If things aren't going well or you are working too hard and all you have in life is your work then it will affect your health.

- To avoid stress or depression you need other things to take your mind off your work. You need a release. This can be anything – catching up with your favourite TV show or just taking time out to rest and reflect.

- Find a hobby or a sport that you enjoy doing for fun.

- Caution beware of continually finding your release in partying and alcohol. This will negatively affect your energy levels and make matters worse, not better. Socialising is good but remember that to be the best at what you do you will need to be refreshed and able to perform at your peak.

The •peoplemad success model

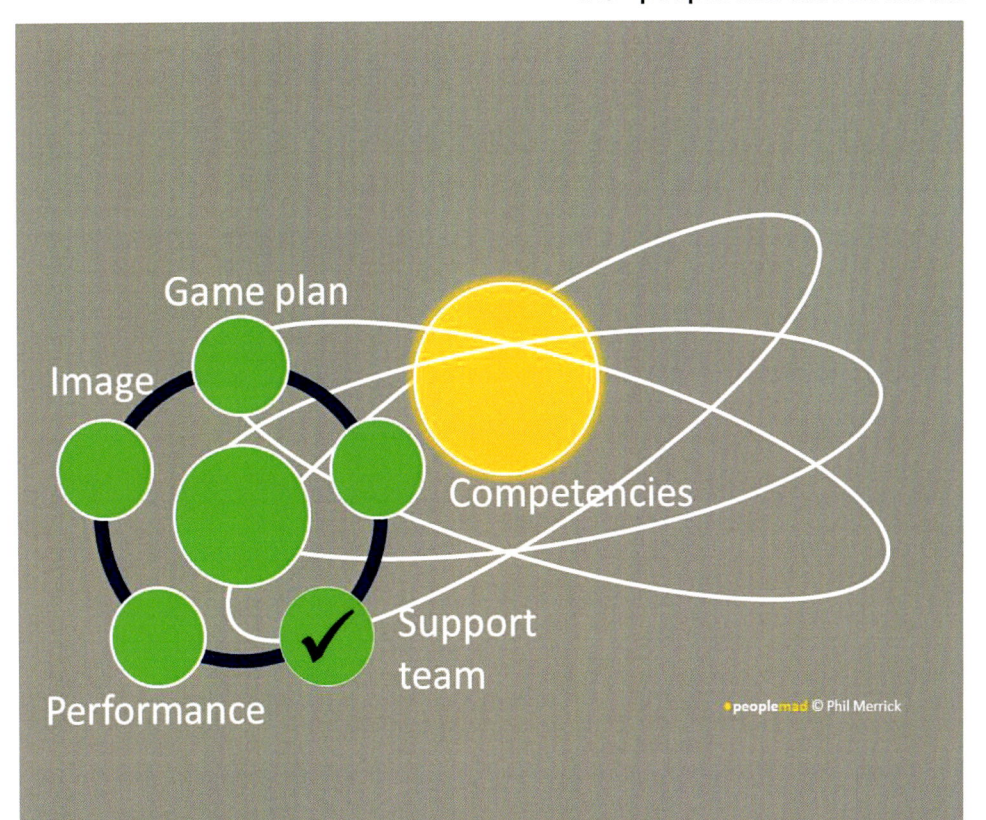

Diagram showing success model with elements: Game plan, Image, Competencies, Support team (checked), Performance

•peoplemad © Phil Merrick

Build your support team

Mentors
Coaches
Managers
P/As
Colleagues
Friends
Family
Advisors

Right people with the right skills, knowledge and experience

The •peoplemad success model

Establish a support structure

- This is about the environment and the people you need to help you achieve your vision, such as Mentors, Coaches, Managers, Personal Assistants etc.
- Surround yourself with the right people:

    –Right attitude:

    100% commitment to the cause.

    Belief in the vision.

    –Right ability:

    Right skills.

    Right knowledge.

    Right experience.

    –Doing the right things:

    All actions focused on the vision.

Create the right environment to enhance your performance:

–In training.

–In work.

–At home.

'No matter what accomplishments you make, somebody helped you.'

Althea Gibson, Black American Grand Slam tennis player.

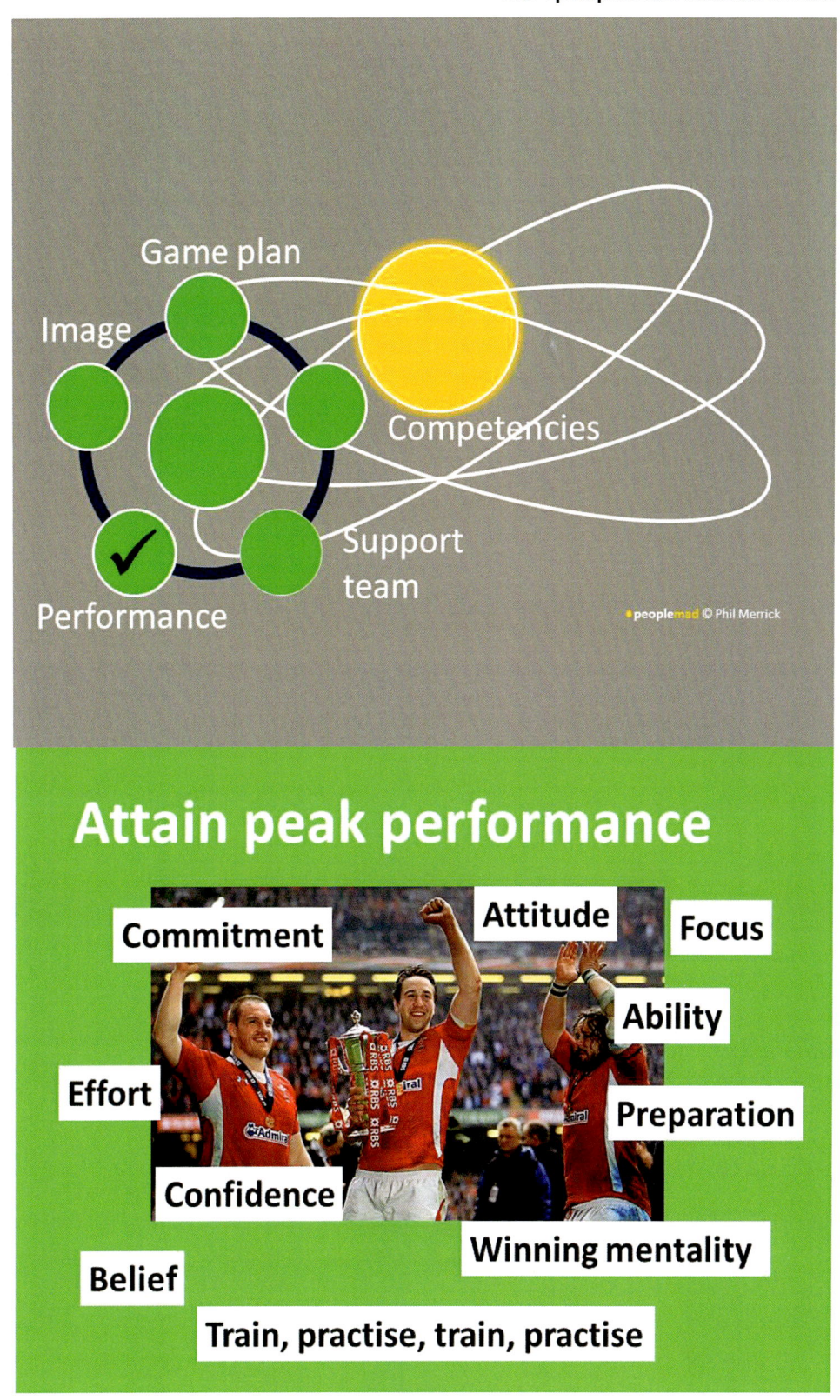

The •peoplemad success model

Game plan
Image
Competencies
Support team
✓
Performance

•peoplemad © Phil Merrick

Attain peak performance

Commitment Attitude Focus
            Ability
Effort   Preparation
Confidence
            Winning mentality
Belief
Train, practise, train, practise

Attain peak performance

Think OUTCOME

This relates to performing 'on the day' from a single task to a complete performance which could take hours.

- Prepare properly beforehand. This will give you the right level of confidence to perform on the day.
- Visualise your performance, see great things happen.
- Do everything you can to feel good about yourself.
- Clear your mind – ready to think about the task in hand.
- Get rid of distraction and disruption.
- Stay focused – concentrate only on the performance.
- During the performance stay in the present:
    - –Don't reflect on mistakes.
    - –Don't look forward thinking what might happen.
- Stay within your comfort zone – don't try things you've not perfected in training.
- Nerves are okay, use them to fire up your performance.
- Stay positive – no negative thoughts whatsoever.
- Stay confident – 'of course I can'.
- When you are winning 'go for the kill'. Stay focussed, don't get complacent, don't ease off. Don't think victory, think *performance.*
- Give 100% effort and enjoy!

'It's all about feeling good about yourself when you go to that start line.'
Iwan Thomas, Olympic silver medallist.

'I don't know why but I have always asked the kit man what colour kit we are wearing, found out what colour the opponents are wearing and visualised scoring goals, or good things happening in the game. I do it before every game, get good thoughts, good moments happening in my head.'
Wayne Rooney, footballer.

'Now you have three more days off – I don't want to see you. Try and go out with friends or family who have nothing to do with this club and switch off. Wednesday morning it's back to work, full on, and the road to Wembley starts.'
Pep Guardiola to the Barcelona players in preparation for the Champions League Final in May 2011. Barcelona beat Manchester United 3-1.

The •peoplemad success model

Some important points

- *To prepare and perform at your very best you must:*
    - *–Keep sight of your vision.*
    - *–Stay positive – don't tolerate negativity.*
    - *–Believe in your ability.*
    - *–Continually stretch your comfort zone in training.*
    - *–Stay within your comfort zone during performance.*
    - *–Practise, practise, practise.*
    - *–Reward success – treat yourself when you've done something well.*

- *Surround yourself with the right people – the people that will help and support you in achieving your vision.*

- *Don't tolerate the wrong people – they will spoil everything for you or at best slow you down.*

- *Work hard, play hard.*

'Be yourself. Everyone else is already taken.'
Oscar Wilde, Irish writer and poet.

The •peoplemad success model

> *Trying to be the best and continually improving performance is one long journey – it never ends and as one destination comes into sight you should set your course for the next.*
> *Follow the model and don't compromise.*

'Keep away from people who try to belittle your ambitions. Small people always do that, but the really great make you feel that you, too, can become great.'
Mark Twain, American writer.

'A genius! For thirty seven years I've practised fourteen hours a day, and now they call me a genius!'
Pablo Sarasate, Spanish violinist and composer.

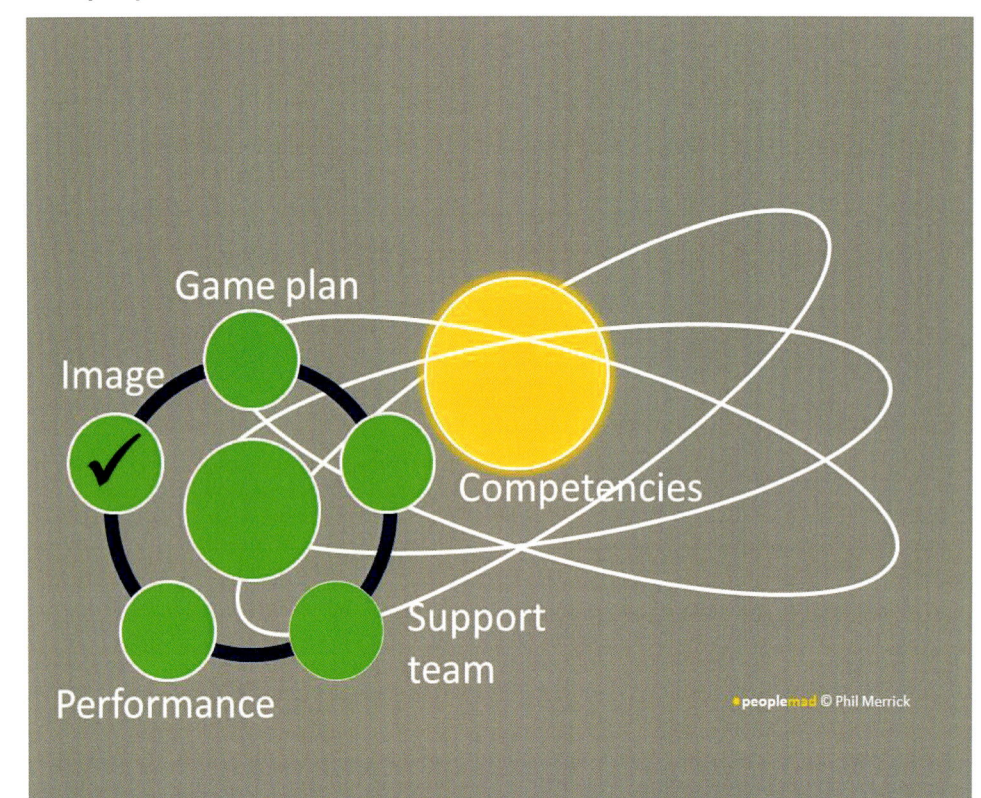

The •peoplemad success model

- Game plan
- Image ✓
- Performance
- Competencies
- Support team

•peoplemad © Phil Merrick

Create the right image

Overall look
Behaviour
Brand
Clothes
Website
Social media
Things you say
People you mix with

232

The ●peoplemad success model

Create the right image

Think OUTCOME

- In it's simplest form 'image' means how you are seen by other people.
- Everyone has an image.
- Do you know how other people see you?
- Is it how you'd like to be seen?
- Image covers everything –
    - Overall look.
    - Behaviour.
    - Brand.
    - Clothes.
    - Website.
    - Social media.
    - Things you say.
    - **People with whom you surround yourself.**
- Choosing the right image can help improve performance by making you feel good about yourself.
- It can also help with your popularity – 'people like dealing with people they like dealing with'.

Think: Dress for the job you want not the one you've got. This is a mind set. Start now. Adopt the image, attitude and behaviour of the person you want to be.

The •peoplemad success model

Your personal action plan

Think OUTCOME

- Get the right attitude.

- Have a strategy and focus on execution.

- Have self belief that you can make things happen.

- Help other people to perform at their best.

- Learn how to influence other people.

- Build your support group.

- Work hard play hard.

- Display leadership.

'Achievement is largely the product of steadily raising one's level of aspiration and expectation.'
Jack Nicklaus, American golfer.

The •**peoplemad** success model

Build capability

Game plan
Image
Competencies
Support team
Performance

•**peoplemad** © Phil Merrick

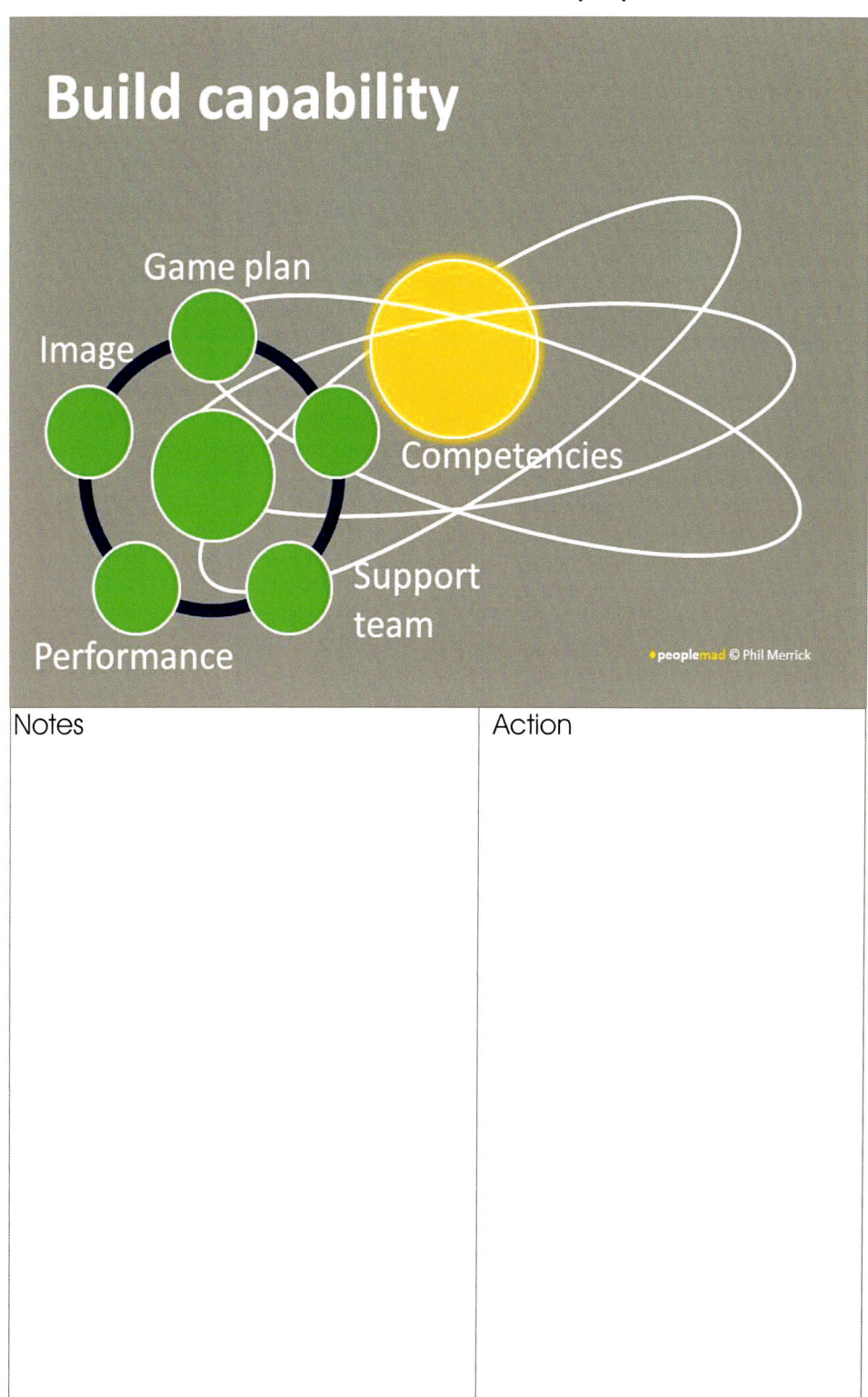

Notes	Action

Your own •**peoplemad** notes

8. Display leadership

In this section:
- The •**peoplemad** success model
- Leadership – the essentials
- Be accountable
- Be accountable: be competent
- Be accountable: make the right decisions
- Have foresight
- Foresight
- Vision
- Give direction
- Inspire others
- Lend support
- People perform best when they feel good about themselves
- Use all of the •**peoplemad** success model
- Dealing with conflict
- Dealing with opposition
- Dealing with setbacks
- Your own •**peoplemad** notes

'A leader has the vision and conviction that a dream can be achieved. He inspires the power and energy to get it done.'
Ralph Lauren, American fashion designer.

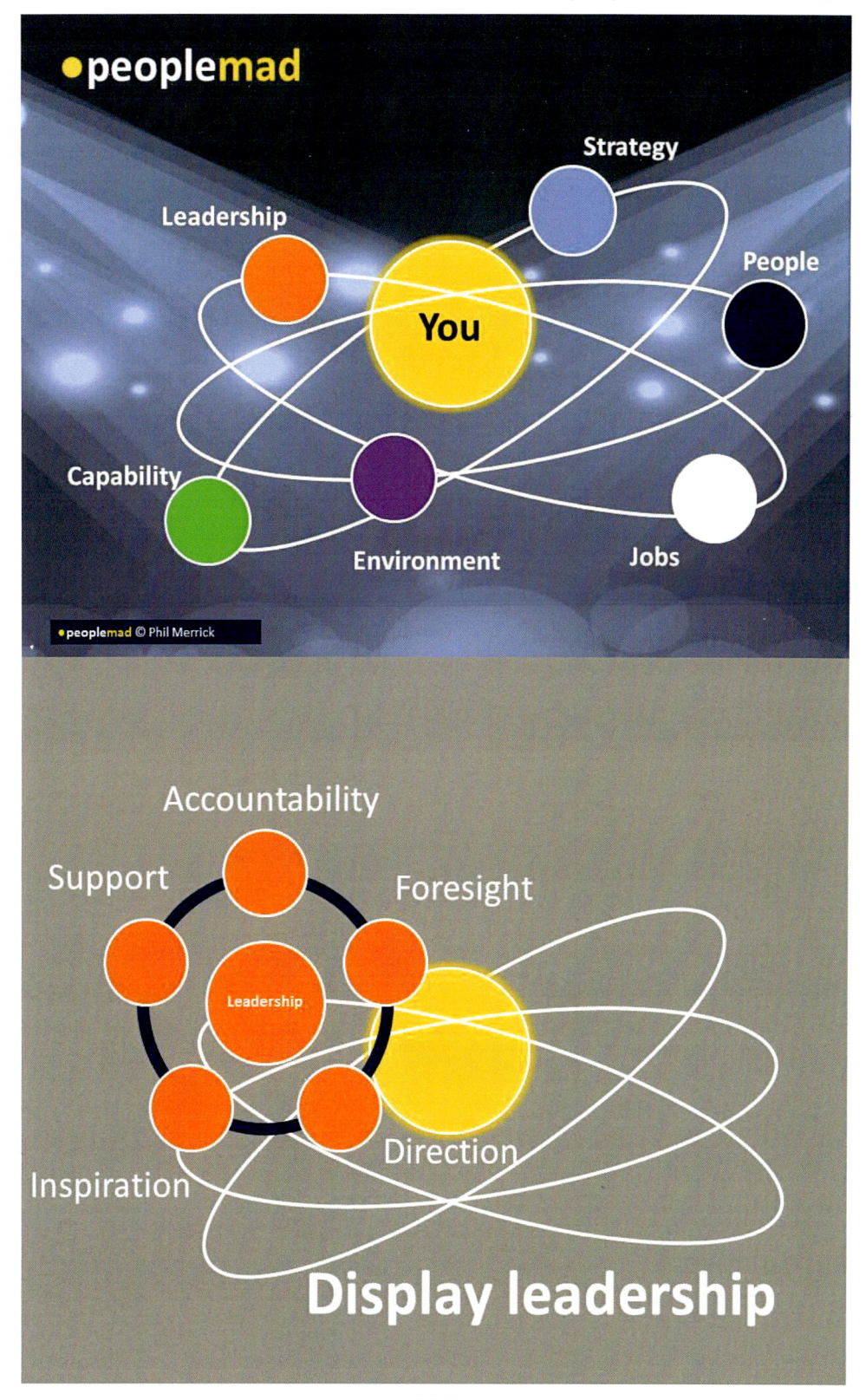

The •peoplemad success model

•peoplemad

Strategy
Leadership
You
People
Capability
Environment
Jobs

•peoplemad © Phil Merrick

Accountability
Support
Foresight
Leadership
Inspiration
Direction

Display leadership

The •peoplemad success model

'The people, and the people alone, are the motive force in the making of World history.'
Mao Tse Tung, Chinese Communist leader.

'In my early years at Aberdeen and Manchester United, I decided right away that in order to build trust and loyalty with the players, I had to give it to them first.'
Sir Alex Ferguson, Manchester United manager, My Autobiography.

'A good leader is a person who takes a little more than his share of the blame and a little less than his share of the credit.'
John C Maxwell, American author.

Leadership is as much about taking control of your life as it is about leading other people – stand up and be counted. You don't have to be a manager to display leadership qualities. Leadership and management are 2 different things. Take ownership of the actions of yourself and your team. Do the right things, direct the actions of others to help achieve the vision. Inspire others through your actions and words. Get people motivated to achieve the vision.

Give help, advice, encouragement; **make people feel good about themselves.** Support them with an open hand. Don't stifle them. Picture the future, create ambition, share the excitement. You can be that person. You don't have to be in charge of people to do those things.

Leadership is about being accountable and taking ownership. Have a purpose to what you say and do – what outcome do you want?

Think carefully about your leadership style. Your actions affect other people, think about what you say and how you say it and the impact you are having on other people's lives.

The •peoplemad success model

Be approachable.

You need to know what's going on in your business – the last thing you want is for colleagues to be frightened of telling you things. And be honest with people, even if the message is a difficult one. If it's not appropriate to say anything then you tell them it's not appropriate. We can all be leaders. Your job is to help other people feel good about themselves. They will then do their jobs better which in turn helps you do your job better.

In November 2005 I went to watch Leeds play Crewe Alexandra at Gresty Road in the Championship – the second tier of English football. Leeds had not long been relegated and were managed by a chap called Kevin Blackwell – his first attempt at being a manager. There's mistake number one by the Leeds United board – a huge club with ambitions to get back into the Premier League and they appoint someone who has never done the job before. Any way we were awful and lost 1-0. I was on my way home listening to Radio Leeds and Kevin came on and said how badly they had played, he criticised the players and said he was going to let them know that he wouldn't tolerate it. Some of them wouldn't be playing for the club again. He distanced himself from the performance. I'm angry, I've told the players, I won't tolerate it.

The •peoplemad success model

On the same evening Chelsea also lost 1-0 to Real Betis and Jose Mourhino the Chelsea manager came on the radio.
We have no defence or argument for it.
We are a great team, we have got to get back to our standards.
We have to look at ourselves to work out what didn't work and try to solve it.
He took ownership – he was accountable – he used the word 'we'.
Kevin blamed the players, Jose didn't blame anyone.
Kevin distanced himself, Jose took ownership.

A few years later Kevin was sacked by Bury and unfortunately still hadn't learnt, publicly calling his players 'garbage'.

Jose Mourhino of course is one of the most successful football leaders in the World.

It is interesting to note, however, that whilst this incident shows his obvious qualities as a leader, he has had his fair share of controversy over the years and has sometimes been accused himself of blaming other people when things don't go his way.

'There is a great man, who makes every man feel small. But the real great man is the man who makes every man feel great.'
G.K. Chesterton, English novelist and critic.

Leadership – the essentials

- Leadership is as much about taking control of your life as it is about leading other people – stand up and be counted.
- Accountability – take ownership of the actions of yourself and your team.
- Foresight – know what lies ahead, picture the future, create ambition, share the excitement.
- Direction – do the right things, direct the actions of others to help achieve the vision.
- Inspiration – inspire others through your actions and words. Get people motivated to achieve the vision.
- Support – give help, advice, encouragement; make people feel good about themselves.

Note:
- Everyone is entitled to their views and opinions – respect this.
- Whatever you say and do will have an impact on somebody's feelings and emotions – people are human beings not robots.

> *'Leadership is about making people feel good about themselves.'*
> **Jose Mourinho, football manager.**

The •peoplemad success model

Accountability
Support
Foresight
Leadership
Direction
Inspiration

•peoplemad © Phil Merrick

Be accountable

Make the right decisions - at the right time

Stand up and be counted

Take responsibility

The •peoplemad success model

Be accountable

- The Oxford English Dictionary definition is: **Required or expected to justify actions or decisions.**
- The **•peoplemad** definition is: taking ownership!
- Leadership is as much about taking control of your life as it is about leading other people.
- Be accountable and take responsibility for your own actions and the actions of your team.
- You don't have to be in charge of something to display leadership qualities.
- Take ownership
    - Don't complain.
    - Don't make excuses.
    - Don't blame other people.
    - Don't put up barriers.
- If things aren't working out do something about it.

The ancient Romans apparently had a tradition. Whenever one of their engineers constructed an arch, as the capstone was hoisted into place, the engineer assumed accountability for his work in the most profound way possible: he stood under the arch.

Be accountable: be competent

- The Oxford English Dictionary definition is: **Having the necessary ability or knowledge to do something successfully.**
- *The trick is in how this ability and knowledge is applied.*
    - –Attitude: *Settled way of thinking or feeling.*
    - –Talent: *Natural aptitude or skill.*
    - –Skill: *The ability to do something well.*
    - –Knowledge: *Information and skills acquired through experience and education.*
- To be a leader there is often a natural expectancy from other people that you know what you're doing.
- You can't be expected to be good at everything and have infinite knowledge. Be honest.
- The trick is using what you do know to act decisively and take the initiative.
- If you don't have sufficient knowledge to make a decision then find it.
- Competence is not finite – your attitude, talent, skill and knowledge are all areas that can be continually improved through effort.
- **Especially decision making – successful leadership depends on it.**

The •peoplemad success model

Be accountable: make the right decisions

Think OUTCOME

- Effective decision making is about achieving the desired outcome.
- Be absolutely clear about the outcome you want.
- Weigh up the pros, cons, risks and impact.
- Don't restrict your thinking; think what would happen if?
- Get all the right information before making a decision.
- Is it accurate? Is it timely? (up to date)
- If you don't have the right information find it.
- It is impossible to be an expert on everything – be honest with yourself about how much you know.
- Use the knowledge and experience of other people.
- Your gut feel saves time and is usually right. This only works if you have the right knowledge and experience. Test it. Make sure it works for you.
- Always think about the impact of your decisions before making them.
- Don't make decisions based on emotion. Take away emotion and make a rational well informed decision.
- If you are still uncertain and you have done all the necessary thinking, analysis and testing then console yourself with the fact that both/all options could work and are likely to achieve a similar outcome.

The •peoplemad success model

An essential quality of Leadership is being accountable and taking responsibility for your own actions and the actions of your team.

'I honestly don't believe I should be here answering questions on behalf of the players. They should be here answering questions on why their performances were so poor, to be honest with you. I don't think it's my responsibility at this stage to answer for a performance as bad as that.'

Stuart Pearce after his England team's poor display in the European U21 Championship. June 2013.

As a football manager you are responsible for picking the team, training them, coaching them on tactics and motivating them. If the players don't deliver how can you distance yourself from their performance? Stuart's contract was not renewed by the F.A.

An unfortunate example.

The •peoplemad success model

- Accountability
- Support
- Foresight
- Leadership
- Direction
- Inspiration

•peoplemad © Phil Merrick

Have foresight

Facts
Experience
Knowledge

Think OUTCOME

Foresight is a skill

Foresight

- The Oxford English Dictionary definition is: **The ability to anticipate future events or requirements.**
- The ability to anticipate future events comes with knowledge and experience – it is not a gift or a supernatural power.
- Get to know your subject matter, your industry, your markets, your surroundings and importantly your people.
- You will get better at this if you continually look ahead and plan the future and then check back to see what happened.
- Compare your expectations with the actual results.
- Practise. Try short term and long term forecasts.
- Watch and listen to the media – read reports.
- Get up to date expert knowledge in your field – become the expert yourself.
- Foresight is a skill. Get good at it.

'Opportunity is missed by most people because it is dressed in overalls and looks like work.'
Thomas Edison, scientist.

Vision

- The Oxford English Dictionary definition is: **The ability to think about or plan the future with imagination or wisdom; a mental image of what the future will or could be like.**

- As a leader people will look to you for direction. You need a clear of vision of what you are trying to achieve in order to point people in the right direction.
- Be passionate about it.
- Get excited by it.
- Get other people excited by it.
- Continually check and ask yourself:
    - Why are we doing it?
    - Is it within reach? It doesn't have to be easy but it needs to feel achievable to keep motivated.

'The very essence of leadership is that you have to have a vision.'
Theodore Hesburgh, American priest.

The •peoplemad success model

Accountability
Support
Foresight
Leadership
Inspiration
Direction

•peoplemad © Phil Merrick

Give direction

Think OUTCOME

Be really good at making decisions

Fly high
Swoop low

Communication
Collaboration
Co-operation

The •peoplemad success model

Give direction

Think OUTCOME

- The Oxford English Dictionary definition is: **The action of directing or managing instructions on how to reach a destination or about how to do something.**
- Encourage communication, collaboration and co-operation.
- Strong leadership is about getting the best results from the other people involved.
- A strong team will have many people with leadership qualities – the trick will be to channel those qualities for the good of the team.
- Don't confuse strong leadership with forcing your will on others – this will just cause resentment.
- Get skilled at making the right decisions at the right time.
- Get to know your subject matter, your industry, your markets, your surroundings and importantly your people.
- Learn to fly high to watch what's going on; learn to fly low, zooming in on what's important.
- Do not be afraid of making difficult decisions.

'Be willing to make decisions. That's the most important quality in a good leader.'
George S. Patton, American general.

The ●peoplemad success model

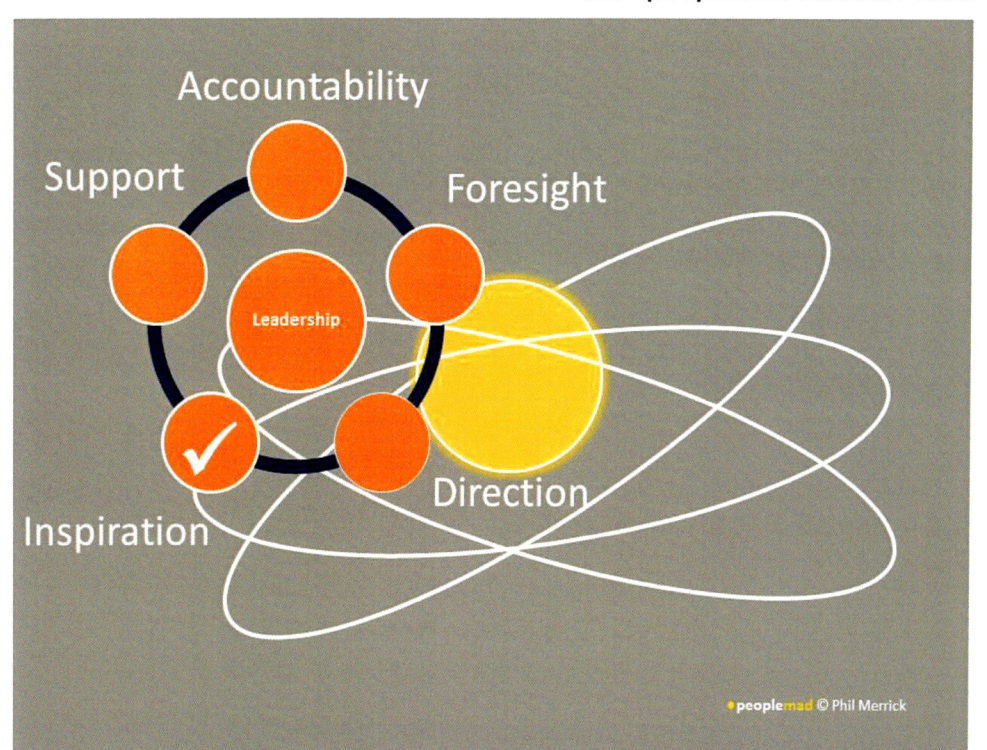

Accountability
Support
Foresight
Leadership
Inspiration
Direction

●peoplemad © Phil Merrick

Inspire others

Through your actions and words

Be the example

The •peoplemad success model

Inspire others

- The Oxford English Dictionary definition is: **Fill with the urge or ability to do or feel something – create a feeling in a person.**
- Be able to inspire others through your actions and behaviour.
- People watch what you do.
- People comment on what you do.
- People copy what you do.
- Do you know how other people see you?
- Is it how you'd like to be seen?
- Think of the impact of your actions on other people, directly and indirectly.
- Get to know your subject matter, your industry, your markets, your surroundings and importantly your people.
- Live and breathe the guiding principles.
- Set an example – be the example.

'You can't wait for inspiration, you have to go after it with a club.'
Jack London, American author.

The ●peoplemad success model

Accountability
Support
Foresight
Leadership
Direction
Inspiration

●peoplemad © Phil Merrick

Lend support

Be actively interested

Empathy
Respect
Dignity

Assistance
Encouragement
Approval
Emotional help

Lend support

- The Oxford English Dictionary definition is: **Give assistance, encouragement, approval, emotional help – be actively interested.**
- Be there for people in times of need.
- Treat everyone with empathy, respect and dignity.
- Give frequent and honest feedback on performance.

Think about your own behaviour:
- Leadership is not about bossing people around.
- Do you ask people to do something for you or do you tell them? Courtesy is to ask.
- Do you say 'I' or 'we'? – you are part of a team it should always be 'we'.
- Do you thank people for doing things? Just because it is someone's job to do something you should still show your appreciation.

- Politeness is a strength and manners are very important.
- Remember - leadership is about making people feel good about themselves.
- Surround yourself with the right people.

The **●peoplemad** success model

People perform best when they feel good about themselves

People feel good about themselves when they:
- Are treated with respect.
- Enjoy what they are doing.
- Know the rules and boundaries within which they operate.
- Know the level of performance that's expected of them.
- Believe in what they are being asked to do.
- Have the right skills, experience and knowledge for the job in hand.
- Are fairly rewarded for their activity and behaviour.
- Can see their contribution to the big picture.
- Feel that they are making a difference.
- Have a sense of belonging.
- Have certainty about their future.
- Like the people with whom they have to live, work and deal.
- Are surrounded by other people who feel good about themselves.
- Are successful at what they do.

'The true way to render ourselves happy is to love our work and find it a pleasure.'
Francoise De Motteville, French writer.

Use all of the •peoplemad success model

- Make people feel good about themselves
- Improve performance

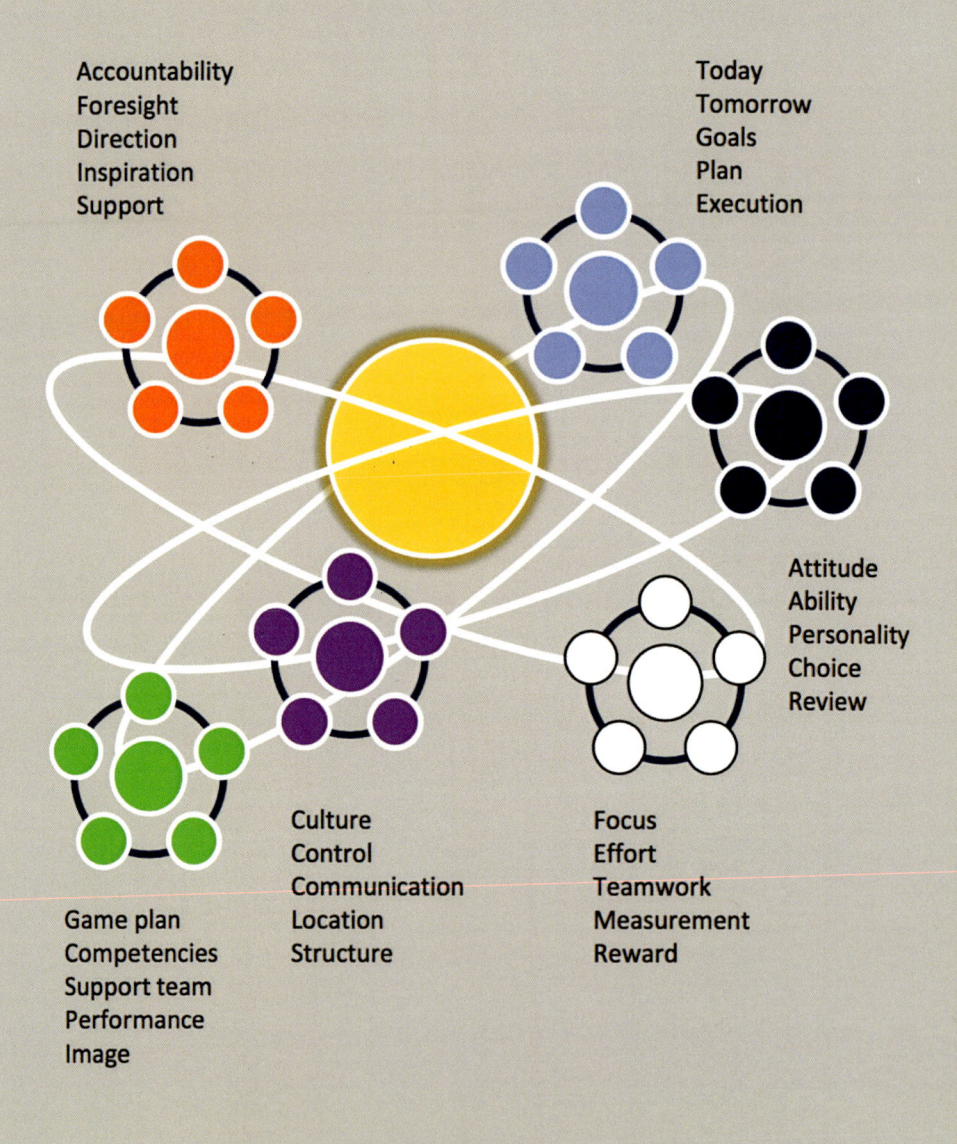

Accountability
Foresight
Direction
Inspiration
Support

Today
Tomorrow
Goals
Plan
Execution

Attitude
Ability
Personality
Choice
Review

Game plan
Competencies
Support team
Performance
Image

Culture
Control
Communication
Location
Structure

Focus
Effort
Teamwork
Measurement
Reward

•peoplemad © Phil Merrick

Dealing with conflict

Think OUTCOME

- Don't shy away from the issue because someone is difficult to deal with – that's what they want.
- Losing your temper does not look or sound good. Stay in an adult state – be the grown up not the child.
- Feel interested not threatened – why do you say that?
- Even if you don't agree with someone you should still be respectful of their views.
- If someone is rude to you don't sink to their level by being rude to them.
- Be firm, be honest, say it as it is.
- Don't waffle, be brief and stick to the facts.
- Take away all the emotions and don't indulge in personal criticism.
- Don't try to belittle someone, it will inflame the situation. It does not make you look big by trying to make someone else look small.
- **Problems fester – deal with them promptly.**
- Stay in control, rise above the situation.
- Look at yourself – are you difficult to deal with? Remember people deal with people they like dealing with.

'No-one can make you feel inferior without your consent.'
Eleanor Roosevelt, Former First Lady of the USA.

The •peoplemad success model

Dealing with opposition

Think OUTCOME

- Keep things simple – don't over complicate your approach.
- Get to know the opposition.
- Nullify their strengths, exploit their weaknesses.
- Make the opposition worry about you.
- Be in control – always.
- Rise above confrontation.
- Listen only to those with the right knowledge and experience.
- Deal with problems promptly – don't let them fester.
- Enjoy the challenge – make it fun.

Stay positive:
- Moaning adds no value whatsoever.
- If you don't like it do something about it.
- Don't worry about things you can do nothing about.
- Don't worry about people who do not affect your World.
- Negativity is draining.
- Look forward – get excited.
- Don't confuse opposition with people who are genuinely concerned about what you are doing and are only trying to help.

Dealing with setbacks

Think OUTCOME

- Setbacks happen. They are part of life.
- Step back, take a moment, gather your thoughts, regroup.
- Understand why it's happened and learn from it.
- Stay positive. Don't complain. Don't make excuses.
- Don't blame other people.
- Don't worry about things you can do nothing about.
- See it as a challenge – how will you recover?
- Think OUTCOME – what's the best way forward?
- Look forward; you can't change what's gone.

This is a good way to think about setbacks:
- The chance of encountering setbacks increases according to the amount of things you do, the harder you try and the more you push the boundaries. To get setbacks you are out there making things happen – well done!
- The only way to completely eliminate setbacks is to stop doing things – not an option if you want to be the best.
- On the journey to achieving what you want there will be lots of setbacks. This is one of them out of the way and you are a step nearer to achieving your goals.

The •peoplemad success model

'Happiness is not the absence of problems but the ability to deal with them.'
Baron de Montesquieu. French political philosopher.

'It takes a great deal of courage to stand up to your enemies, but even more to stand up to your friends.'
J.K. Rowling, author.

'The art of leadership is saying no, not yes. It is very easy to say yes.' **Tony Blair, British Prime Minister.**

'Leadership is the priceless gift that you earn from the people who work for you. I have to earn the right to that gift and have to continuously re-earn that right.'
Sir John Harvey-Jones, Chairman of ICI.

The ●**peoplemad** success model

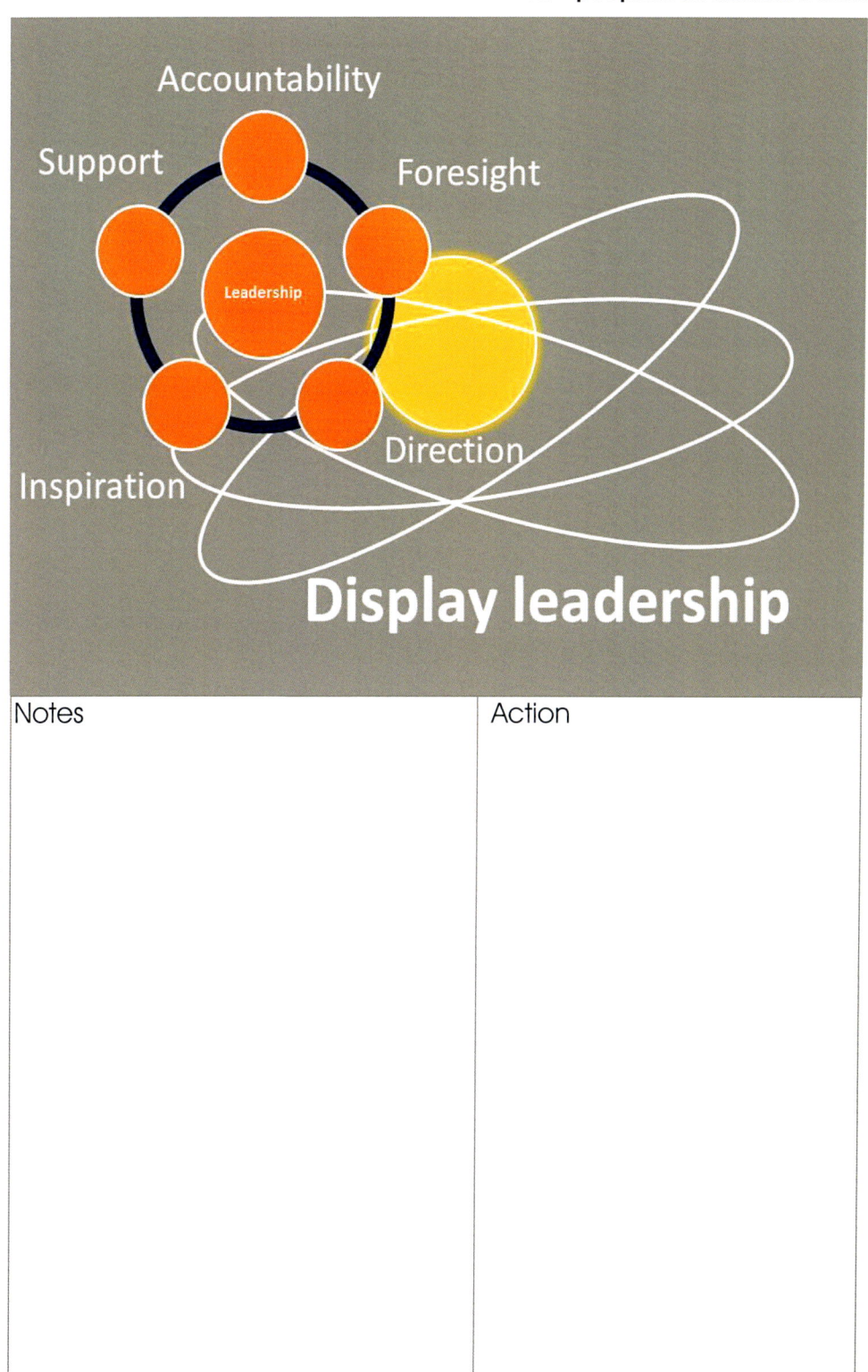

Accountability
Support
Foresight
Leadership
Inspiration
Direction

Display leadership

Notes	Action

Your own ●**peoplemad** notes

9. The •peoplemad tool kit

In this section:
- You determine the OUTCOME
- Think Impact
- Look at *everything relative to everything else*
- The Relativity Pie chart
- An example of a Relativity Pie chart
- Relativity traffic lights
- An example: personal performance
- Think of the importance before rating
- *Today Tomorrow* thinking
- The *Today Tomorrow thinking picture*
- Prioritising tasks
- The prioritising tasks picture
- Your own •peoplemad notes

This tool kit is very much about how you think about things. Look at things differently to make informed decisions on where to focus your efforts and improve performance.

'The best way to predict your future is to create it.'
Peter F. Drucker, Management consultant, author.

You determine the OUTCOME

- Things happen in your life caused by the interaction of you with other people.
- Some things will be good, some will be bad – this is life, accept this is how it works.
- When things happen they have a direct impact on your life.
- The scale of that impact is not determined by the event itself but by how you choose to deal with it – how you think and the actions you take.

- **Y + P = O**

Think OUTCOME

How you deal with other people will determine the outcome.

- Take control.
- Decide how you want to think about the event – does it matter?
- Decide what OUTCOME you want.
- Consider your actions.
- Take the appropriate steps to deliver your desired outcome.
- Think FORCED OUTCOME – work out how to force the outcome you want from something e.g. events, meetings, negotiations.

Think Impact

- Whenever you do something it has an impact.
- Think about who and/or what is affected?
- How big is the impact?
- Do you know whether it has a positive or a negative impact?
- Before you took the action did you pre plan the impact you wanted to make?
- Look at what you are doing every day – are you making an impact?
- Is it the right impact?
- Is it aligned to your strategy – what you want to achieve?
- Link IMPACT to OUTCOME. What outcome do you want? What is the impact being made as a consequence of that outcome?
- How do you measure your impact and that of your team?
- Refer to the Measurement pages in Section 5 to get some ideas.
- Think effectiveness, think quality.
- Continually assess what you do and the impact you're making and use the findings to make improvements to your overall performance.

Look at everything relative to *everything else*

- 'Being the best' as a statement assumes relativity to something else. You will only be the winner if you are better than somebody else.
- To win you need to do everything you can to improve your capability and understand the capability of the competition.
- In direct competition your capability will need to include *strategic and tactical skills to beat your opponent (such as exploiting their weaknesses).
- Look at your strengths and weaknesses relative to each other. What's important? Where should I focus?
- Look at your skills relative to each other – which one's contribute most to your performance? Which one's should contribute most?
- Look at your team's performance – best performer?
- Look at your business performance – best area?
- Look at how you spend your time – is it spent on what's important to you?

*Strategic is high level longer term planning, tactical is short term, doing things now.
Think: strategy to win the war, tactics to win the battle.
Think: strategy to win the league, tactics to win the match.

The Relativity Pie chart

- Use a simple pie chart to show things relative to each other.
- Think of a full pie as 100%.
- Show your items as percentages of the whole.
- This is not meant to be a science.
- Guesstimates work well.
- The point is to get you thinking about the relativity.
- **Some suggested uses are:**
    - –Time spent on things
    - –People who influence you most
    - –Things that are Important to you
    - –People who are contributing to something
    - –Your skill set
- Use it to improve your own performance and redraw the pie every so often to see what's changed. For example, you might want to spend more time with your staff, so something else needs to change.

An example of a Relativity Pie chart

Chart how you spend your time then chart what's important to you and check you are focused on the right things.

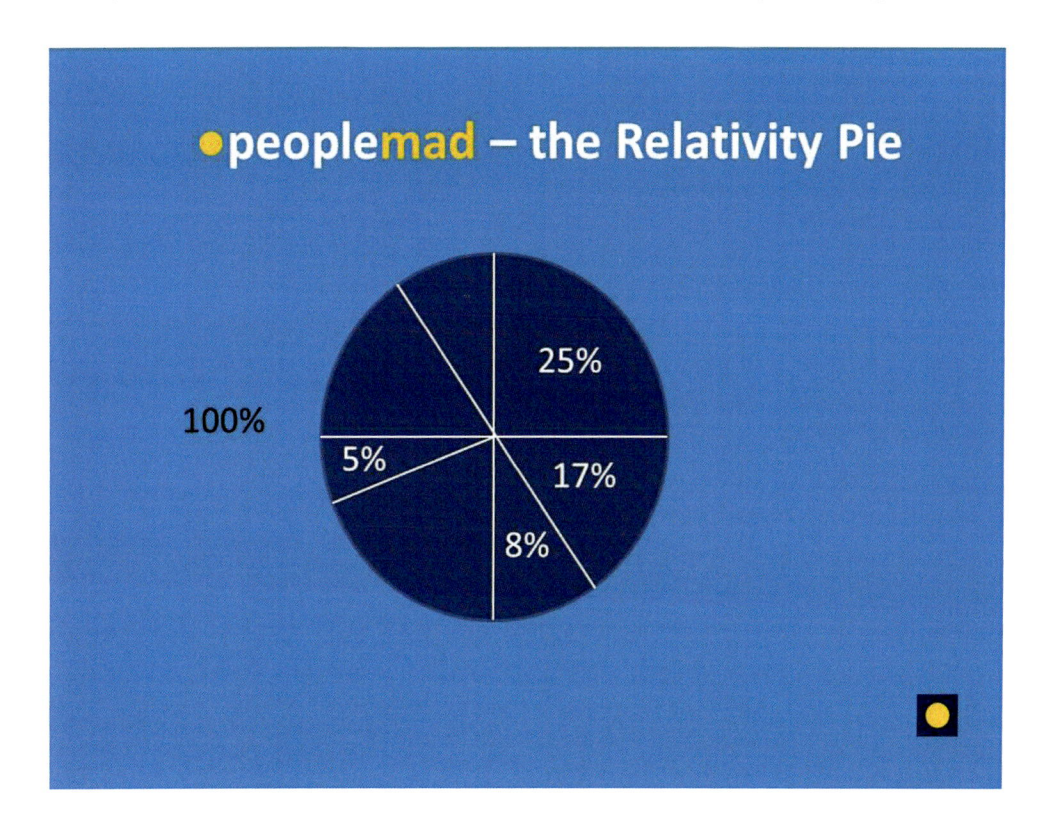

•peoplemad – the Relativity Pie

100% — 25%, 5%, 17%, 8%

Use the Relativity Pie to create 'space'. How do I spend my time? What can I stop doing? Create space, give yourself more time, reduce unnecessary hassle. Keep things simple.

Relativity traffic lights

1 (green) **2** (yellow) **3** (red)

No attention needed	Needs attention	Needs urgent attention
Low priority	Medium priority	High priority
Strong performance	Average performance	Weak performance
Low risk	Medium risk	High Risk

The relativity traffic lights are a quick and easy way to look at what needs doing and where you should focus your efforts. Detailed scoring systems with a greater range of values have their place but for many things they over complicate something which can often be quite simple. If it needs attention it needs attention. Keep it simple.

Use this in conjunction with the task prioritisation model at the end of this section to decide what needs to be done first.

•peoplemad rating personal performance

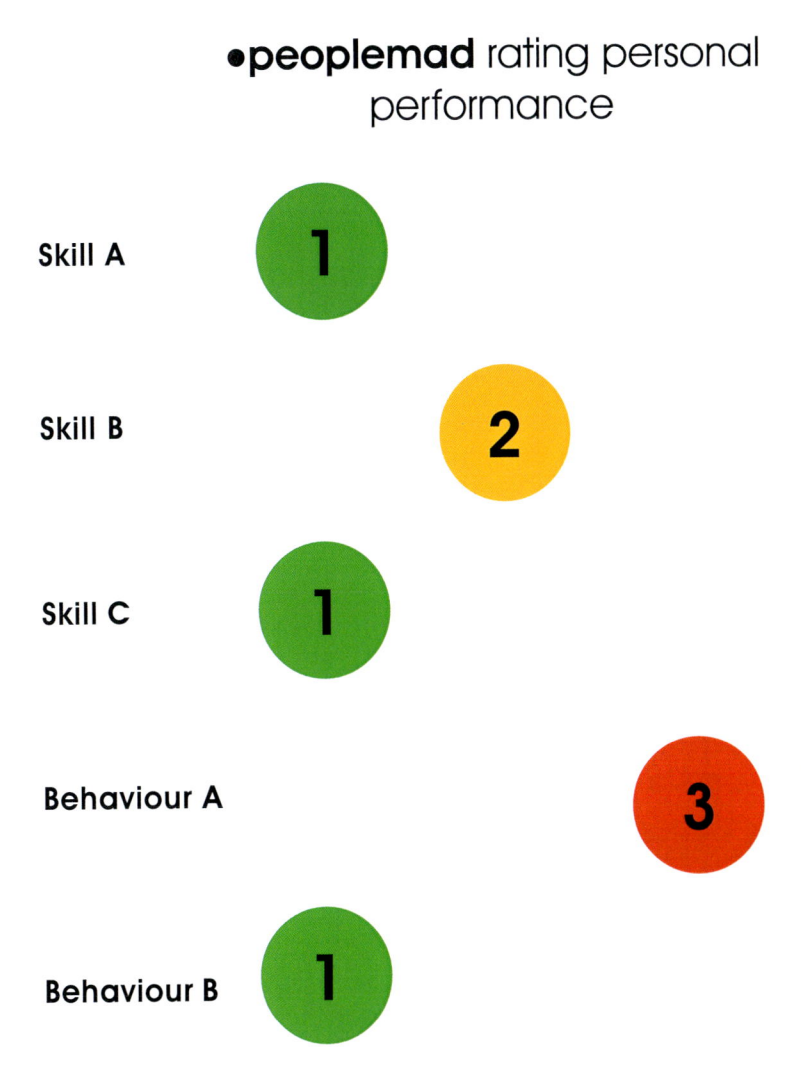

Skill A	🟢 1
Skill B	🟡 2
Skill C	🟢 1
Behaviour A	🔴 3
Behaviour B	🟢 1

Relativity Traffic Lights can be used for rating anything – e.g risk assessment, the performance of business areas and processes. They can also be used as a heat map to give a quick overview of progress on activity.

Think of the importance before rating

- Not everything has the same importance.
- When you are rating things relative to each other always consider the importance – mentally giving things a 'weighting'.
- For example there is no point rating a skill as red and in need of urgent attention if it is not an area that is important in your development.
- This might seem obvious but get into the habit of thinking importance first then relativity. So if it is not important then it gets a green because even though it might be a weak area for you it does not need attention.
- The definitions provided in the rating chart allow for this, for example a green rating signifies low priority, no attention needed, a yellow needs attention and red needs urgent attention.
- Where you then have a number of items in the same category, for example yellow needing attention, you can prioritise them according to importance and ease of carrying them out (see Prioritising tasks).

'If the choice lies between the production or purchase of two commodities, the value of one is measured by the sacrifice of going without the other.' **H.J. Davenport, economist.**

Today Tomorrow **thinking**

- You will have noticed that Today Tomorrow thinking is a technique used frequently in ●**peoplemad**. This is because it is key to improving performance which is what ●**peoplemad** is all about.
- The detail of Today Tomorrow thinking is given in Section 3 Develop your strategy and Section 7 Build your capability.
- The technique can be used for long term and short term planning.
- It works particularly well with career/ life planning and improving performance over a long period of time.
- It also works with short term projects – getting fit, losing weight, building your capability.
- What does today look like?
- What do I want tomorrow to look like?
- What are the actions I need to take to move from today to tomorrow?
- Prioritise and timeline the actions – plan.

The •peoplemad success model

The Today Tomorrow thinking picture

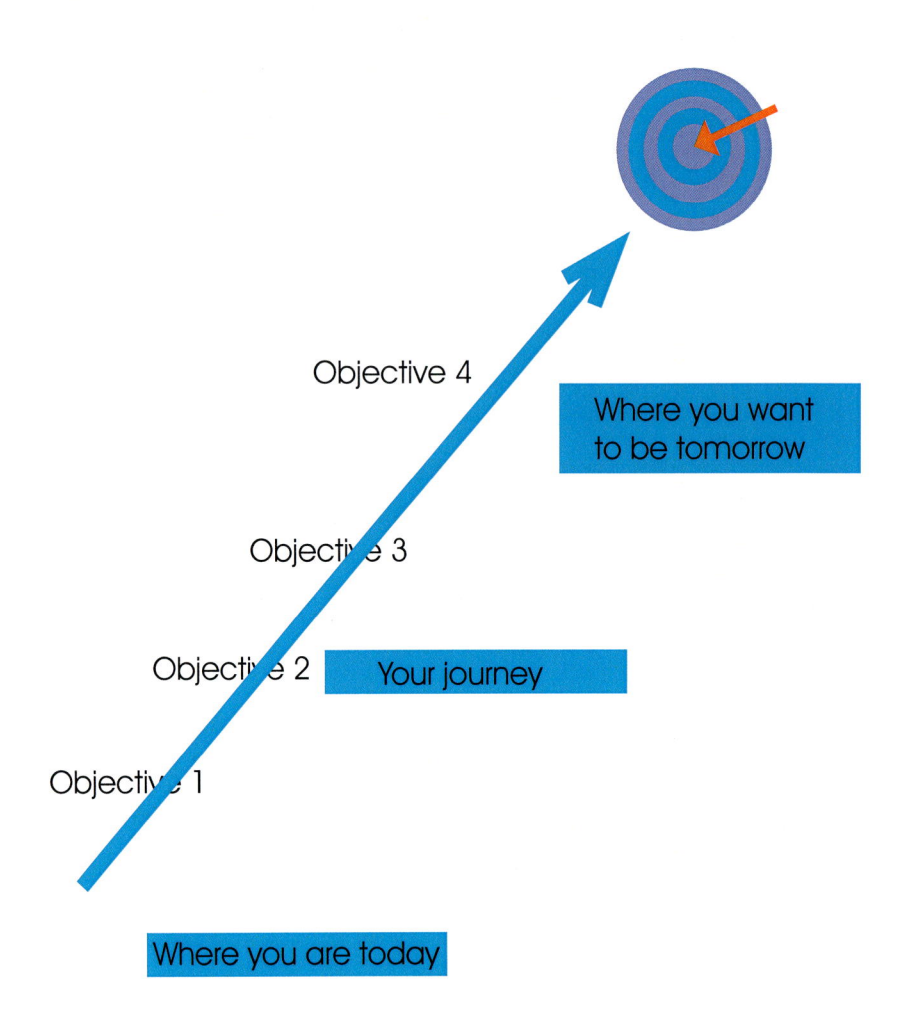

Objective 4

Where you want to be tomorrow

Objective 3

Objective 2   Your journey

Objective 1

Where you are today

•peoplemad © Phil Merrick

The ●peoplemad success model

Prioritising tasks

Think OUTCOME

- Make sure that you get the right balance between time spent planning and the time spent doing things.
- Don't rush into things – you will make mistakes and waste a lot of time undoing or correcting things.
- Efficiency is about doing things in the right order at the right time for the right length of time and this needs planning.
- The flip side of this is that you don't want to spend too much time deliberating where to start. Every second you spend planning is not being spent on taking action.
- In a competitive situation you could be leaving a window of opportunity open for someone to 'get in there first'.
- A quick way to prioritise tasks is tackle the important ones first and the ones that are the easiest to carry out – see diagram.

Important note:
- If things are desperate and urgent action needs to be taken then think how do I plug the holes in a sinking ship? This will quickly identify what needs doing first then when you've stopped the leaks you can move on to all the other things that need doing.

The •peoplemad success model

The prioritising tasks picture

Create an action plan starting with what's important and relatively easy to correct

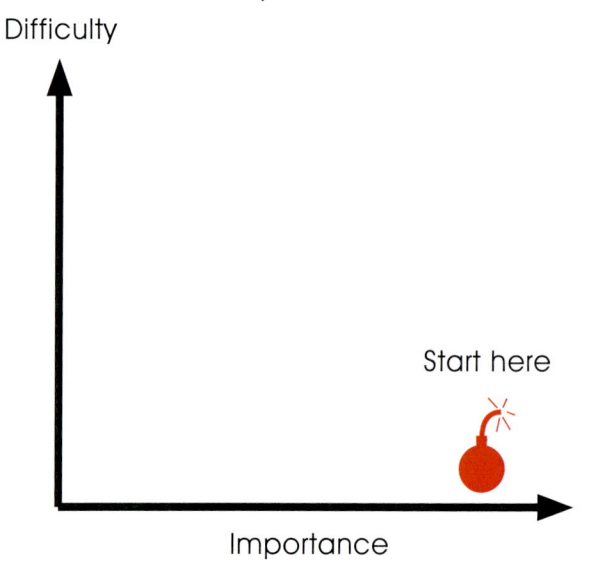

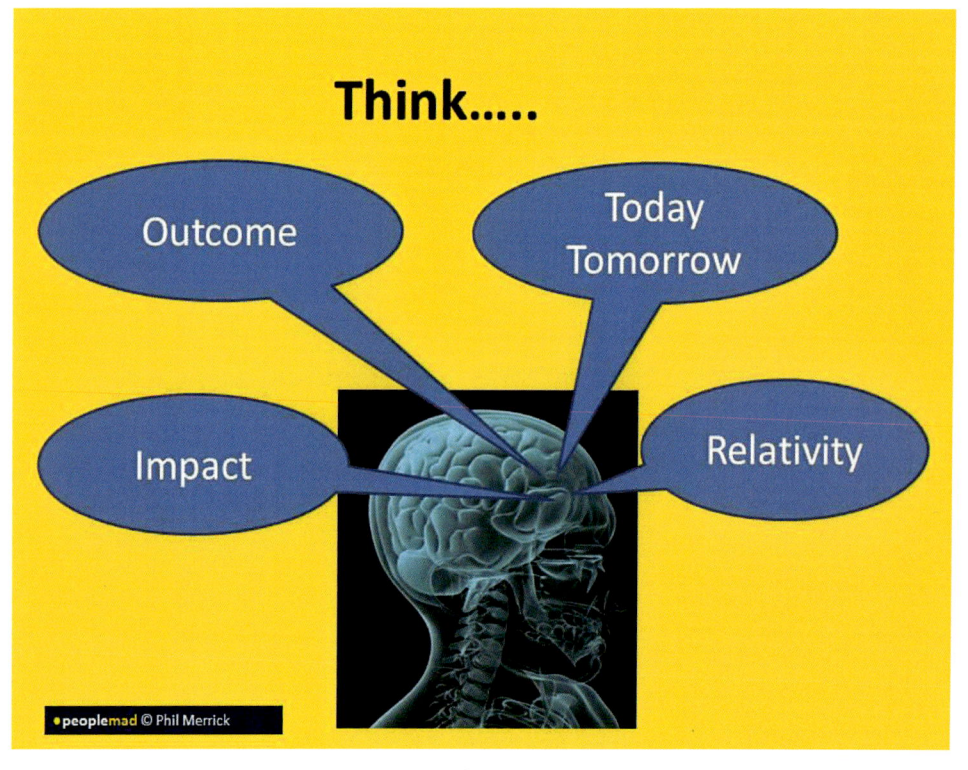

Difficulty

Start here

Importance

Think.....

- Outcome
- Today Tomorrow
- Impact
- Relativity

•peoplemad © Phil Merrick

The •**peoplemad** success model

Notes	Action

Your own •**peoplemad** notes

10. How you can use •peoplemad

In this section:
- The benefits of using •peoplemad
- Use the model for anything
- Setting up something from scratch
- Reviewing and improving performance
- Brief notes on assessing performance
- Brief notes on managing change
- Developing individuals
- Personal life
- Your own •peoplemad notes

'I had a hard time working hard when I was younger and eventually when I figured out why am I doing all the fitness, why am I working hard on a tennis court it all of a sudden started to flow. I was getting to balls I didn't know were possible to get to and also just sort of believing that I can pull off miraculous shots and all that and I made it pretty fluid. I don't know where that came from but I realised I was able to play like this at the highest of levels and I'm happy I chose to go down that route of working unbelievably hard.'

Roger Federer, Swiss Grand Slam tennis player. June 2014.

The •peoplemad success model

Use the model for anything

Including :	
Setting up a new venture / project	✓
Reviewing performance	✓
Troubleshooting	✓
Change management	✓
Training your teams	✓
Managing your teams	✓
Career and life coaching	✓
Personal development	✓

The essential tool kit to improve performance
- for everyone, everywhere

•peoplemad © Phil Merrick

The •peoplemad success model

Setting up something from scratch

OUTCOME / Think

Use the 6 planets as the key components of your methodology:

- Develop your strategy.
- Surround yourself with the right people.
- Get the right people doing the right things.
- Create the right environment.
- Build your own capability.
- Display leadership.

Follow this handbook from the need for a vision in Section 3 through to creating the right environment and the development of your people in Sections 6, 7 & 8.

In very simple terms:

- Know what you're aiming to achieve and get the right people on board.

- Get them doing the right things in an environment that will allow them to flourish and perform at their very best.

- Build your own capability and display strong leadership at all times.

Reviewing and improving performance

- The basic principles and rules of •**peoplemad** can be used to assess where you are today and whether your business is adequately structured to allow for continuous improvement.
- This also applies to individuals and what they need to do to improve personal performance.
- Carry out a review using the headings from the different sections in this hand book.
- For the performance of your team or organisation concentrate on Sections 3 to 6.
- For your own performance or to review the personal performance of a colleague concentrate on Sections 2, 7 & 8.
- Identify those weaknesses that need to be improved.
- Use a simple rating system to document your assessments, see Section 9 .
- Remember some areas are more important than others.
- Create an action plan.
- **The most important action point will be making sure you've got the right people around you.**

Brief notes on assessing performance

- Start an assessment with an open mind – clear your head of any pre conceived ideas.
- Whilst your gut feeling is usually right be careful not to let it influence your approach to the assessment. There is the risk that subconsciously you will try to prove your gut feeling right.
- Do your assessment and assess it fairly and rationally – then check to see if your gut feeling was near the mark.
- Use a rating system that suits you – the traffic light system in Section 9 is quick and can be as accurate as you want it to be. Importantly it's simple to use and prioritises what you need to focus on, which is the whole point of the exercise.
- Record brief notes as to why you've given the scores.
- Keep it simple.
- Continually monitor the success of your rating system and adjust it accordingly.
- Assessment is made easier if you have something to assess against – e.g. previous expectations, targets, objectives.
- Refresh your expectations after each assessment.
- Spend your time wisely: performance is improved with action not analysis which is just a means to an end.

Brief notes on managing change

- To improve performance you have to be prepared to change.
- Change requires a move from one state to another – this particularly applies to your state of mind.
- You need to win the hearts and minds of others – successful change requires the alignment of attitudes of those involved and impacted.
- The ideal starting point is 100% dissatisfaction with the status quo – be mindful that this is unlikely to happen.
- Constant, effective communication is critical.
- Change is disruptive – it needs a great deal of thought to make sure everything has been considered.
- It needs careful planning, including the time needed to bed in.
- Sometimes you will need to take a step backwards in order to take two steps forwards.
- Similarly change can cause a dip in performance before improved performance kicks in. This needs to be managed carefully to prevent it from happening or at least minimise the impact.
- Put monitoring processes in place – stay close to figures, activity and the **people.**

The •peoplemad success model

Developing individuals

Think OUTCOME

- Whether working as part of a team or performing on their own encourage people to take ownership of their career and personal development.

- Clarify their vision.
- Devise a strategy.
- Carry out self analysis – today versus tomorrow.
- Set some objectives.
- Develop a plan.
- Get the right attitude.
- Build their capability.
- Establish a support structure.
- Create the right image.
- Attain peak performance.

'Everyone thinks about changing the World but no one thinks of changing himself.' **Leo Tolstoy, Russian writer.**

Personal life

Think OUTCOME

- Stick to the •**peoplemad** rules.
- Have ambition – look forward, get excited.
- Have a plan for what you want to achieve.
- You are who you mix with.
- You need to surround yourself with the right people – those with the right attitude.
- Watch and learn from other people – find a role model.
- Make sure you do the right jobs that give you the right experience for what you want to do as a career.
- Do the things that you enjoy doing – you will be good at them.
- You need to work in an environment that allows you to flourish.
- Display leadership qualities at all times.
- Take control – don't let other people control your life.
- Don't compromise your values – ever.
- Lose the wrong people – now. It's their loss not yours.
- Caution do not surround yourself with 'yes' people who just say what you want to hear.

The •peoplemad success model

Notes	Action

Your own •peoplemad notes

11. A quick summary

In this section:
- The •**peoplemad** rules in brief
- The •**peoplemad** success model
- Each planet has 5 moons
- The •**peoplemad** tools in brief
- Your own •**peoplemad** notes

'Work seven days a week and nothing can stop you.'
Sir John Moores, British businessman.

'People will only change if they see where that change is taking them.'
Adam Crozier, Royal Mail.

'Knowledge is power.'
Francis Bacon, English writer, philosopher and statesman.

The •peoplemad rules in brief

1. Believe in yourself
    - Attitude is everything
    - You can achieve what you believe you can achieve
    - You are in control of what you think and what you do

2. Surround yourself with the right people
    - You rely on other people every day
    - The power of many is greater than the power of one
    - Use other peoples' skills to complement yours

3. Keep things simple
    - Easier to understand
    - Easier to communicate
    - Less to go wrong

'What you're supposed to do when you don't like a thing is change it. If you can't change it, change the way you think about it. Don't complain.'
Maya Angelou, African-American author.

•peoplemad © Phil Merrick

The •peoplemad success model

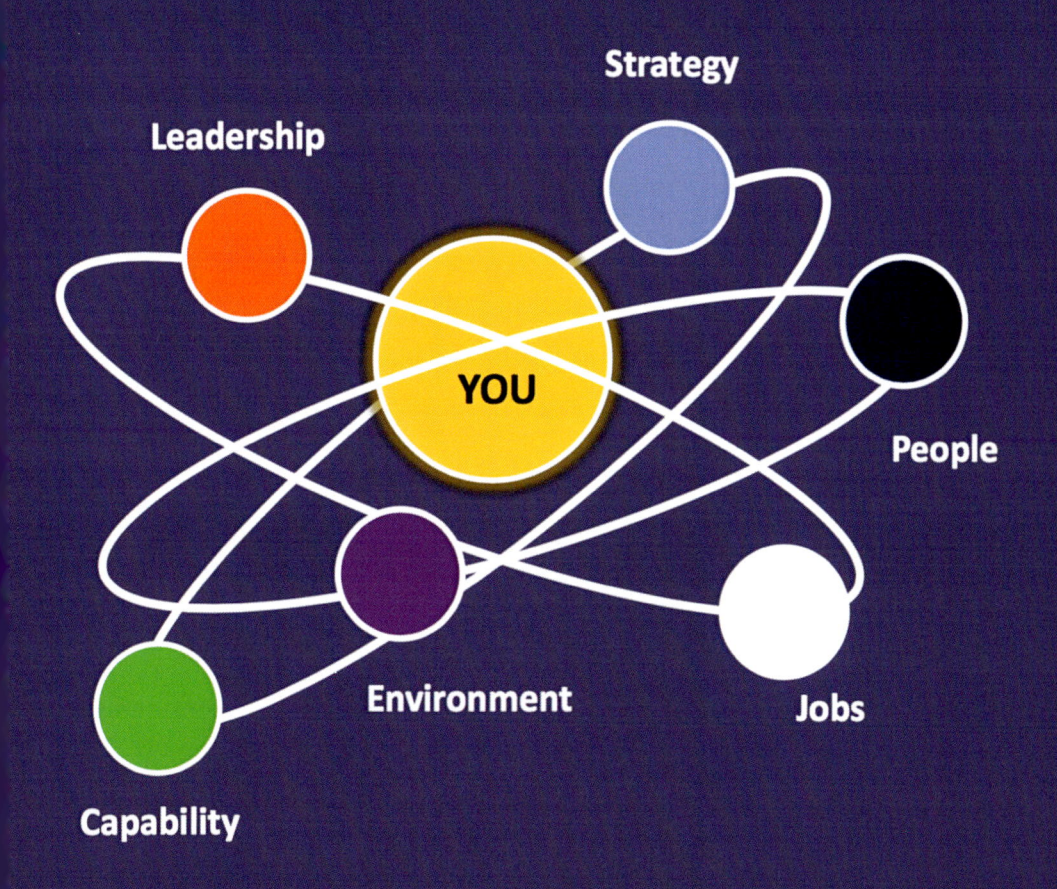

- Strategy
- Leadership
- YOU
- People
- Capability
- Environment
- Jobs

•peoplemad © Phil Merrick

Each planet has 5 moons

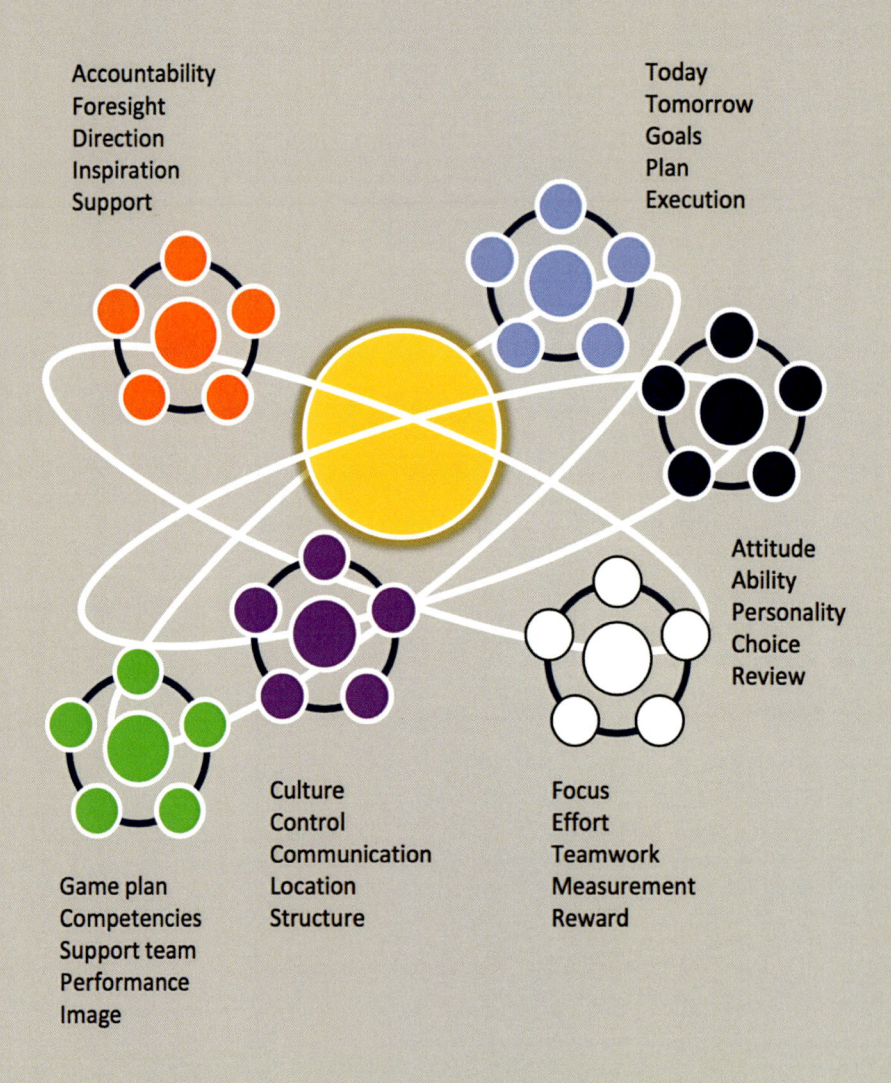

Accountability
Foresight
Direction
Inspiration
Support

Today
Tomorrow
Goals
Plan
Execution

Attitude
Ability
Personality
Choice
Review

Game plan
Competencies
Support team
Performance
Image

Culture
Control
Communication
Location
Structure

Focus
Effort
Teamwork
Measurement
Reward

•people**mad** © Phil Merrick

The •peoplemad tools in brief

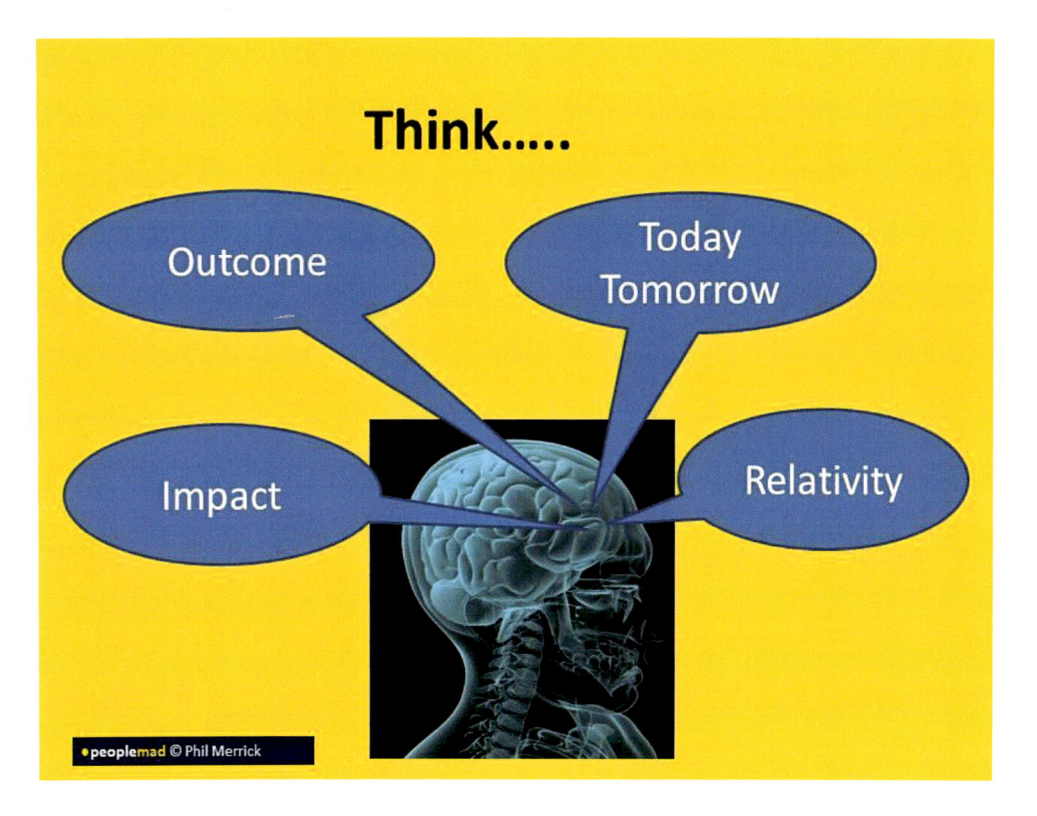

Think.....

- Outcome
- Today Tomorrow
- Impact
- Relativity

Think OUTCOME. Y+P=O.

- *How you deal with other people will determine the outcome. Take control.*
- *Decide how you want to think about the event.*
- *Decide what OUTCOME you want.*
- *Consider your actions.*
- **Take the appropriate steps to deliver your desired outcome.*

The •peoplemad tools in brief continued…

Think IMPACT
- What impact am I making?
- Is it the desired impact?
- Link Impact to Outcome – what do I want to achieve? What impact do I want it to have?

Think TODAY TOMORROW
- What does today look like?
- What do I want tomorrow to look like?
- What are the actions I need to take to move from today to tomorrow?
- *Prioritise and timeline the actions – plan.

Think RELATIVITY
- Look at everything relative to everything else.
- 'Being the best' is a relative statement. You will only be the winner if you are better than somebody else.
- To win do everything you can to improve your capability and understand the capability of the competition.

***Think about the relative importance of something before prioritising and taking action.**

The •peoplemad success model

Get into the •peoplemad habit

•peoplemad © Phil Merrick

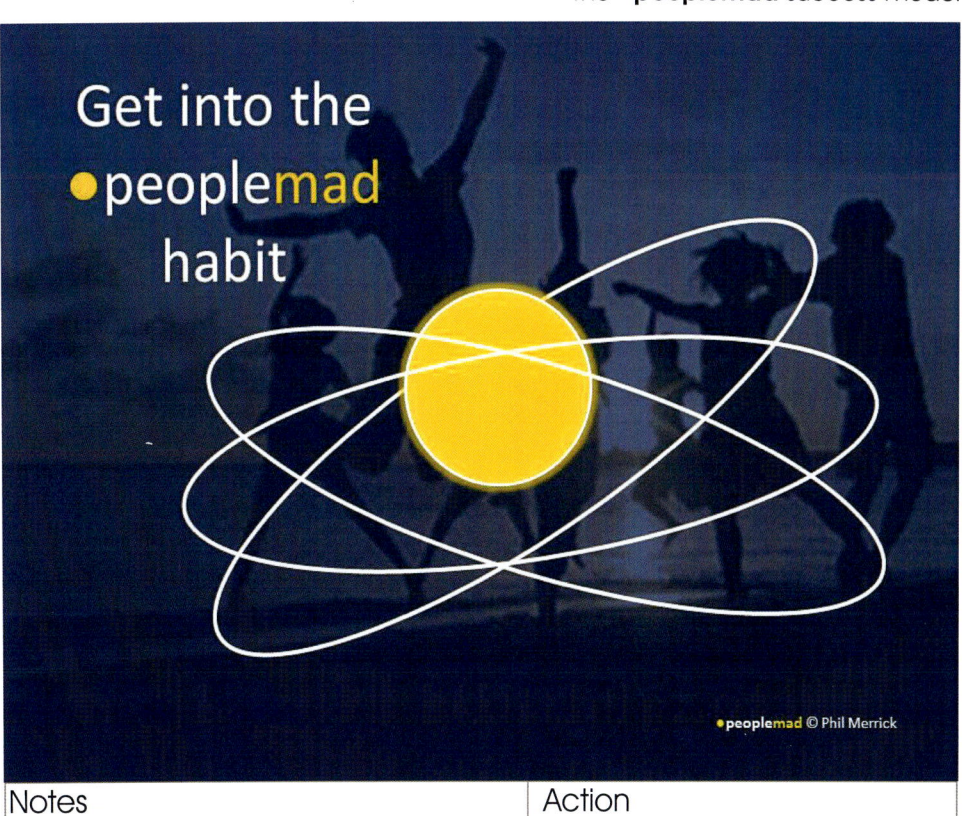

Notes	Action

Your own •peoplemad notes

The •peoplemad success model

Believe in yourself
Surround yourself with the right people
Keep things simple

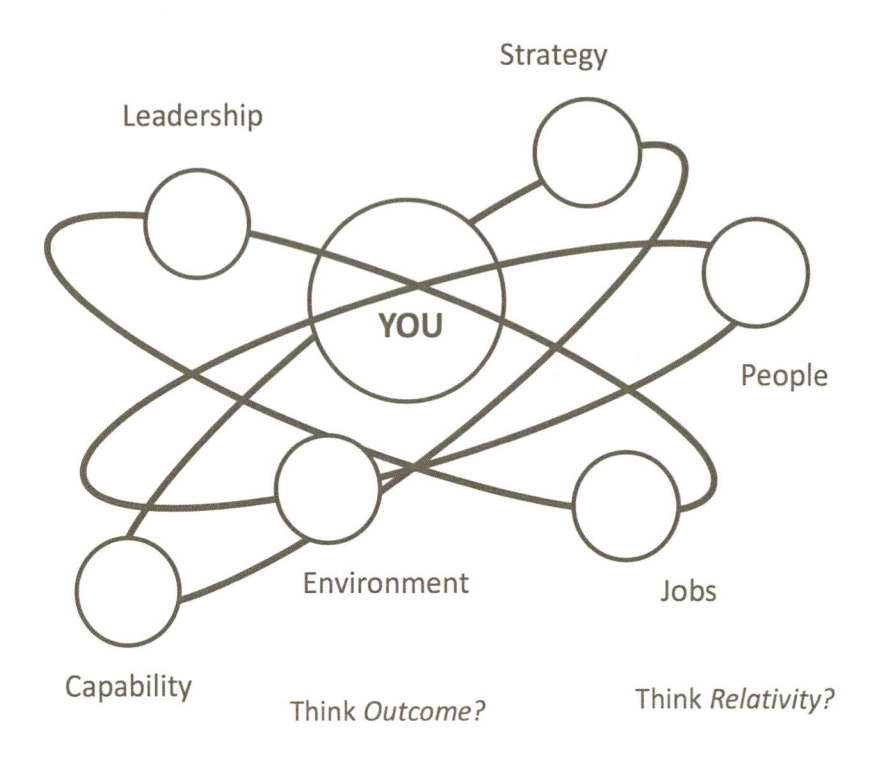

Strategy
Leadership

YOU

People

Capability   Environment   Jobs

Think *Outcome?*   Think *Relativity?*

Think *Impact?*

Think *Today... Tomorrow?*

•peoplemad © Phil Merrick

The •peoplemad success model

A foundation on which to build success
– everything you need in one model

- Important principles
- Simple techniques
- Easy to use
- Easy to remember
- VERY EFFECTIVE

•peoplemad © ....be the best
www.peoplemad.com